INTENTIONAL
DISRUPTION

Leadership Lessons in Healthcare, Business, and Beyond

INTENTIONAL
DISRUPTION

Benjamin Breier

ForbesBooks

All proceeds from the sale of this book will be donated to the Kindred HOPE Fund, a 501(c)(3) charitable organization dedicated to helping any Kindred employee who has experienced a devastating loss or traumatic event in their life.

Published by ForbesBooks, Charleston, South Carolina.
Member of Advantage Media Group.

ForbesBooks is a registered trademark, and the ForbesBooks colophon is a trademark of Forbes Media, LLC.

Printed in the United States of America.

10 9 8 7 6 5 4 3 2 1

ISBN: 978-1-94663-380-4
LCCN: 2021901086

Cover design by David Taylor.
Layout design by Wesley Strickland.

This custom publication is intended to provide accurate information and the opinions of the author in regard to the subject matter covered. It is sold with the understanding that the publisher, Advantage|ForbesBooks, is not engaged in rendering legal, financial, or professional services of any kind. If legal advice or other expert assistance is required, the reader is advised to seek the services of a competent professional.

 Advantage Media Group is proud to be a part of the Tree Neutral® program. Tree Neutral offsets the number of trees consumed in the production and printing of this book by taking proactive steps such as planting trees in direct proportion to the number of trees used to print books. To learn more about Tree Neutral, please visit **www.treeneutral.com**.

Since 1917, Forbes has remained steadfast in its mission to serve as the defining voice of entrepreneurial capitalism. ForbesBooks, launched in 2016 through a partnership with Advantage Media Group, furthers that aim by helping business and thought leaders bring their stories, passion, and knowledge to the forefront in custom books. Opinions expressed by ForbesBooks authors are their own. To be considered for publication, please visit **www.forbesbooks.com**.

To my mother, Neelie Breier, we love you always and in all ways.

CONTENTS

ABOUT THE AUTHOR

BENJAMIN A. BREIER is the chief executive officer of Kindred Healthcare LLC. He became CEO in March of 2015, after having been named president in 2012.

In July 2018, Breier led a consortium of buyers, including Humana; TPG Capital; and Welsh, Carson, Anderson & Stowe in a successful leveraged buyout of previously publicly traded Kindred Healthcare (NYSE:KND). Prior to taking the company private, Kindred had revenues in excess of $7.5 billion, 110,000 employees, and operations in forty-seven states and served more than one million patients per year.

Throughout Mr. Breier's tenure at Kindred, he has strategically deployed capital to create leading scaled businesses in a variety of areas. Acquiring and integrating publicly traded RehabCare in 2011 made Kindred the largest rehabilitation provider in the United States; acquiring and integrating Gentiva Health Services in 2015 made Kindred the largest provider of home health and hospice in the country. In 2017, Breier completed the divestiture of one of the largest skilled nursing facility platforms, completely exiting the skilled nursing industry. Breier also oversaw the acquisition of Centerre in

2015, creating one of the nation's largest inpatient rehabilitation facility platforms.

Breier received his bachelor's degree in economics from the Wharton School of Business at the University of Pennsylvania. He received both an MBA and an MHA from the University of Miami.

Breier serves on the board of Kindred Healthcare and the Federation of American Hospitals and is a member of the Wall Street Journal CEO Council. He also serves on the board of the University of Miami's School of Business, the board of overseers at the University of Pennsylvania, and the University of Louisville Health board of directors. He chairs the Louisville Healthcare CEO Council.

Modern Healthcare magazine named Breier one of the 100 Most Influential People in Healthcare on three occasions and in 2010 recognized him as one of the young leaders aged forty and under making a difference in healthcare. *Louisville Business First* named Breier the Health Care Leader of the Year in 2015 and in 2018 named him the Excellence in Business Leadership honoree.

FOREWORD

EACH YEAR WE work with hundreds of CEOs, corporate boards, and political leaders through Yale University's Chief Executive Leadership Institute, executive retreats, and personal engagements. We find a striking congruence between our leadership research, the topics we focus on in our programs, and the challenges raised by senior executives in the real world.

Today, more than ever, the most salient questions involve how to lead in an increasingly uncertain and disruptive business, political, and societal environment. How can leaders sustain organizational growth and excellence without reeling from crisis to crisis in a reactive way? How can leaders be proactive and define their destiny and not have it handed to them?

An alum of one of our CEO programs, Benjamin Breier has tackled this challenge head-on and written a compelling book, *Intentional Disruption!* He does so from his perch as CEO of Kindred Healthcare, a Fortune 500 company that has faced more than its fair share of existential challenges, both from unpredictable, exogenous factors and through internal tests.

Using a wide range of business research, practical experience, and an earlier stint as an elite college baseball player, Breier argues convincingly that CEOs and business leaders can control their destiny in an unpredictable world. Intentional disruption is a leadership approach that purposively counteracts external forces and ultimately drives predictable business success in volatile times.

Let's be clear, Breier is hardly the first to recognize the potential that harnessing the power of disruption holds for business success. Breier builds on a solid conceptual foundation. In 1942, economist Joseph Schumpeter popularized the phrase "creative destruction" to describe his theory that continuous innovation is necessary for enterprises to survive in capitalist markets where complacency can doom a business into obsolescence.

Even when things are going well, Schumpeter urges organizations to systematically tear down and redefine existing systems, processes, and products. Create. Destroy. Repeat. This is the central dogma of Schumpeterian economics, and it's followed by a growing wave of CEOs looking to sustain competitive advantage in a world that's nearly impossible to forecast. But it's easier said than done. Just ask any chief executive. It requires a certain kind of leader who can make sense out of constant chaos.

Breier's book gives us the help we need.

What is unique about Breier's book is that it's a series of authentic and compelling personal stories that in aggregate provide the reader with a practical view for how to use intentional disruption as a proactive leadership strategy. It does so by providing a contextual roadmap and then bringing each step to life by recounting disruptive events faced by Breier: media threats, legislative threats, natural disasters, shareholder actions, and complex business transactions.

But Breier is careful to point out that intentional disruption is no panacea. We are heartened that this book confronts head-on the risks and challenges of being a disruptive leader—professional, organizational, personal—and makes very clear that this approach is not for the faint at heart. Breier emphasizes that disruption can be hard for even the most confident leader. Imagine ripping out the machinery of success in a high-octane company that's experiencing consistent profitability and then replacing it with an entirely new and unproven engine that hasn't been road tested. But that's exactly what intentional disruption requires. Courage is a prerequisite. And that's just the start.

Our own research has revealed that becoming a disrupter isn't only about attitude or leadership style. Instead, the core building blocks of any disruptive leader are empathy, self-awareness, passion, integrity, resilience, and judgment. It's the combination of *all* these leadership skills that enable disruptive leaders. Take just one away, and the entire house of cards comes tumbling down.

Without resilience, there's little chance a leader can bounce back from inevitable setbacks that are going to surface when introducing new change initiatives. Without empathy, leaders can't step into the shoes of multiple stakeholders to build consensus around strategic initiatives, particularly disruptive ones. Without self-awareness and intellectual curiosity, leaders risk getting stuck in risk-averse ways of thinking, blinding themselves to bold actions that might be required for growth. And without integrity, nothing else really matters for leaders, especially disruptive leaders.

Over the years we've personally watched Breier navigate Kindred through a death trap of seemingly insurmountable obstacles. Intentional disruption works for Breier because he has the courage needed to disrupt *and* he possesses the underlying leadership skills needed to follow through and bring to life the disruptive strategies. In our opinion, that's why he was the perfect person to write this book. We recommend *Intentional Disruption* to CEOs, board members, and rising star leaders in business, academia, and government. It's an entertaining read. Yet it is also highly practical and built on a solid conceptual foundation.

Jeffrey A. Sonnenfeld

Yale School of Management Senior Associate Dean for Leadership Studies & Lester Crown Professor in the Practice of Management

Jeffrey Cohn

CEO advisor and frequent contributor to *Harvard Business Review*, *The Wall Street Journal*, and CNBC

INTRODUCTION

ONLY A NAIVE BUSINESS LEADER would set the unrealistic goal of becoming the chief executive officer of a Fortune 500, New York Stock Exchange, publicly traded company. Only an idealistic kid playing Little League baseball on the warm, sunny fields of Miami, Florida, would dream of making it to the major leagues. Call me naive and idealistic, but I grew up with aspirations of both.

Any reasonable person looking at the odds of accomplishing either lofty ambition would recognize that only 750 athletes get to play at the highest levels of professional baseball—a .015 percent chance. Only five hundred business leaders become CEOs of Fortune 500 companies—an even smaller percentage. Despite a successful run in baseball, I failed to make it to the major leagues. I did, however, beat the odds and make it to the "big leagues" of business when I became the CEO of Kindred Healthcare, Inc., a Fortune 500 healthcare company based in Louisville, Kentucky.

Though I wasn't aware in my youth of my burgeoning leadership skills, I did know from a young age on the baseball field that I didn't just sit back and let things come at me—instead, I went after them. Even though I never made it to the highest levels of professional baseball, I would one day use the leadership skills and toughness I harnessed on the field and incorporate them into my business leadership strategy.

INTENTIONAL DISRUPTION ON THE BASEBALL DIAMOND

It was 1981, and I was ten years old sitting in the car beside my father, sharing a seemingly insignificant conversation. We were stopped at a red light on a street near our Miami home when my father first mentioned a baseball Little League in Perrine, Florida, about thirty minutes south. My father and I had always played baseball together. I don't know if he was a skilled player, but he was an avid enthusiast. He grew up in New York, and like most New Yorkers, he was a Yankees fan. He had begun to teach me the game at an early age. We talked often about strategies and players, and we practiced together daily. I think that more than anything, I loved baseball because it allowed me more time with my dad.

Sometime around the age of eight, it became clear that baseball was going to be as important to me as it was to him. At this young age, I certainly didn't know where the sport might take me, but baseball came naturally to me, and like most kids that age, this was enough to interest me. In fact, I loved the game so much that my parents had a batting cage built on a sliver of land in our backyard, and they even had a pitching machine installed. I practiced in that batting cage twice a day every day until I left home for college.

At that stoplight with my father, after his casual mention of the new league, he told me about the recent Mariel boatlift, a mass emigration of Cubans that resulted in almost 125,000 refugees reaching Florida. Many ended up staying in South Florida, and some wound up in the town of Perrine. Anyone who knows anything about baseball knows that many of the best professionals come from Latin America. The Perrine Khoury League had become one of the most talented and competitive leagues in the area. For this reason, my dad was offering me the option to switch leagues.

I had been playing baseball for several years in a league called Howard Palmetto, which was a few minutes from my house. Most of the kids I played with looked like me and talked like me. We went to the same school and had similar backgrounds and home lives. On the contrary, many of the families in places like Cutler Ridge and Hialeah were from a different country and even spoke a different language. I knew I would be considered an outsider if I transitioned to a new league. For a ten-year-old, it was scary to think about leaving a comfortable situation to try something new.

My family and I debated for a while and talked it over with my coaches, who ultimately encouraged me to give it a shot. If I did make the decision to transfer to this new, tougher league, my parents said they'd figure out how to make the hour-long commute possible. Friends in my neighborhood asked why I wanted to join a different league. I didn't have answers; I just knew I wanted to challenge myself. I imagined the players in Perrine to be tougher, more hard-nosed. This interested me, and I thought I might like to learn to play baseball in that style.

After careful consideration, I decided to make the move. I remember being nervous when I arrived because I didn't know anyone, but I didn't let it affect my game. Perhaps in part because of my family's example, I always had confidence in my ability to figure things out. This came in handy when the other kids were speaking Spanish; any performance anxieties I had were eclipsed by the need to decipher what these players and coaches were saying.

I tried to focus on my job as a catcher that day. I had always been a catcher. Many kids didn't like the position because it required heavy gear and crouching down in the hot Florida sun. I always liked it, though, because I could see the whole field. I felt like I was in charge, calling the pitches, setting the defenses, and rallying the troops. As it turns out, it was probably an early sign that I would one day excel at leadership positions; at the time, however, I just understood that I was innately drawn to it.

The transition proved easier than I thought. Fortunately, I learned how to speak passable Spanish pretty quickly while acquiring a new style of play and integrating myself into a new peer group. Despite my underlying insecurities during tryouts that first day, I wound up being one of the top players in that year's draft. I was excited and ready to learn as much as I could.

The choice to join the Perrine League turned out to be massively important in terms of my own confidence and athletic trajectory. It not only put me on a path toward accomplishing many things in baseball but also allowed me to start seeing the world as a young teenager. In fact, I was invited by the Khoury League to play for Team USA, which allowed me at age thirteen to tour Japan and play in Tokyo during an international championship that we ultimately won.

I could not have predicted the path my life would one day take, but looking back, there were early signs of the adult I would become. I'm the first to admit, I'm a high-strung guy. I took daily batting practice until my hands were raw, and I tended to overprepare for games. I'd run through plays continually in an attempt to ready myself for the unforeseen.

Despite my pregame nerves, however, I found that when I stepped between the lines, I was calm. My process in the boardroom is much the same: I overprepare for meetings; I run through every scenario; I plan every detail. By the time the meeting starts or the deal is happening, I am as calm as I was on the field. My formative sports experiences trained me to be a game-day player and leader on and off the field.

I realized early that my decision to leave what was familiar to challenge myself with the unfamiliar was the catalyst for opportunities I could not have imagined. In fact, not long ago as president and chief executive officer at Kindred Healthcare, I was leading a meeting with a businessman whose company we were considering acquiring when he mentioned he knew me. It turned out, he, too, had played baseball and knew of my experience in Miami. This connection cemented the meeting's success and created an ongoing business opportunity.

After my experience in the Perrine Khoury League, I vowed to remember the critical relationship between disruption and success and to never turn down an opportunity just because it seemed challenging or intimidating. In fact, I was determined to put myself in these situations more often. Joining the Perrine Khoury League was my first intentionally disruptive decision, and though it pulled me from my comfort zone, it led to tremendous opportunities and rewards throughout my life. I would come to learn that being intentionally disruptive would be an important business strategy, as a means of producing growth and value and as a way to counter disruptions by external forces.

INTENTIONAL DISRUPTION AS A BUSINESS STRATEGY

I worked incredibly hard to put myself in position to become CEO of one of the largest healthcare services companies in the world by the age of forty-four. As you will discover in these pages, the path toward this achievement did not come from a straight line of victories; nor did it come without many challenges along the way. With each challenge or disruption I faced, I used the strategy that continues to drive my success: intentional disruption, a bold, purposeful, personal and business strategy to create opportunities and kindle successes while counteracting the inevitable disruptions wrought by external forces that can thwart the best-crafted plans and goals.

Using disruption as a business and leadership strategy is not a new concept. Joseph Schumpeter, an Austrian-trained economist and economic historian developed a theory he called "creative destruction," which names the process by which new realities—like new technologies, new products, new processes, new methods of production—make old ones obsolete. This destructive force has the potential to drive innovation and evolution, but it also has the capacity to force existing companies to either quickly adapt to the new environment or fail. In his book *Capitalism, Socialism and Democracy*, he asserts that

> *practically any investment entails, as a necessary complement of entrepreneurial action, certain safeguarding activities such as insuring or hedging. Long-range investing under rapidly changing conditions, especially under conditions that change or may change at any moment under the impact of new commodities and technologies, is like shooting at a target that is not only indistinct but moving—and moving jerkily at that.*[1]

Though his book was originally published in 1942, his theories are timeless and are as applicable in modern society as they were in Schumpeter's day. These same "creative destructions" continue to test leaders and companies. Without intentional strategies to navigate

---

1   Joseph A. Schumpeter, *Capitalism, Socialism and Democracy* (New York: Harper Perennial, 2008), 88.

emerging technologies and disruptions, businesses can become obsolete. For this reason, leaders must develop skills and tools—despite their unique, innate dispositions—to counteract forces that are capable of destroying their companies and their future leadership opportunities.

Though Schumpeter's ideas are not new, the contemporary equivalent of his "creative destruction theory" is what I call intentional disruption. I have always viewed myself as an intentionally disruptive leader. Throughout my life, when I found myself in difficult situations, I would make daring, intentionally disruptive decisions to counteract obstacles I faced. These actions did not come without risks, as I would discover in 2017, when—seemingly at the top of my game—I was forced to counteract the most difficult disruptions I had ever experienced.

During this time, Kindred was attempting a complex leveraged buyout (LBO), also known as a go-private or outright sale of the company's then-public assets. I was working to manage one of the most complicated multiple-party deals ever attempted in the healthcare services space. At the same time I was navigating the transaction with a multitude of counterparties, I was engaged with my board of directors, my 115,000 Kindred teammates, my public shareholders, and my young family in an effort to keep things stable while under the intense public scrutiny that Yale's Jeffrey Sonnenfeld once warned of: "A consequence of seeking a leadership position is being put under intense public scrutiny, being held to high standards, and enhancing a reputation that is constantly under threat."[2] Little did I know during that fateful year that my own intentional disruption strategy would

---

2   Jeffrey A. Sonnenfeld and Andrew Ward, *Firing Back: How Great Leaders Rebound after Career Disasters* (Boston: Harvard Business School Publishing, 2007), 168.

be disturbed in its own right by three disparate circumstances: an act of God, an act of government, and an act of greed.

When I found myself as a new CEO attempting a complicated transaction, I realized that my entire life—athletically, personally, and professionally—had led to this moment of intentional disruption. Had I not honed my strategy and been aggressive in its execution, I am not sure Kindred, or my place at its helm, would have survived.

Our culture moves at a frenetic pace. Once your feet hit the floor in the morning, even the best-laid plans for the day can go awry with one email, text, or tweet.

Disruption in our modern world arrives in the form of geopolitical conflicts, domestic politics, financial and economic news, personal or family crises, professional stresses, government regulations, and, of course, global health pandemics. Considering the speed at which these conflicts reach us through social media and digital access, we can easily be overwhelmed by external forces.

Since we are living through one of the most disruptive periods in our nation's history, it has spawned a recent trend of leadership books exploring ways to manage chaos. Let me be clear: this is not a book about disruption; rather, it's about being intentionally disruptive in business, leadership, and life. For this reason, the book will be divided into three parts to help readers discern how intentional disruption can be used in all facets of life:

- **Part 1, "Clearing the Path for Intentional Disruption."** As a leader, you will undoubtedly be disrupted by external events. In this section, I will explore the types of disturbances leaders encounter and ways to clear the path for intentional disruptions as a proactive strategy to chart the path that you and your organization can take.

- **Part 2, "Leading with Intentional Disruption."** The most successful leaders are proactive rather than reactive. In this section, you will learn how to transition from being disrupted to being disruptive in purposeful and constructive ways.

- **Part 3, "Managing the Effects of Intentional Disruption."** Being intentionally disruptive does not come without risks to one's team, family, health, and integrity. This section will help you protect yourself and others from unbridled chaos so that you can remain focused and intentional about your strategies.

Throughout the book, I will use real-life, hard-fought examples as an athlete and a CEO of how I've used intentional disruption to advance my career and to cultivate my life. Though I will lean heavily on my baseball training and the lessons it instilled, all sports and creative disciplines can provide lifelong leadership lessons, as I've witnessed through my sister's competitive swimming and my daughter's field hockey training. Baseball certainly isn't the only path to leadership, but since it was my path, I share it throughout these pages. Likewise, healthcare is not the only arena for disruptive leadership. Whether you're the leader of a large corporation, a small business owner, or an aspiring entrepreneur, you are not immune. Everyone has experienced disruption. But not everyone has learned how to harness the power of disruption to fuel opportunity and kindle success.

Using real-time examples of my innate disposition as an intentionally disruptive leader, this book addresses the following questions about how leaders deal with disruptions in their jobs and in their personal lives:

- Are you an intentionally disruptive individual?

- How does an intentionally disruptive leader deal with the external disruptions that can upend an organization?

- When is taking aggressive, offensive action the clearest and most definitive path for an intentionally disruptive leader?

- How can an intentionally disruptive leader bring along others on their team to see the true value of changing the status quo?

- How important is it for intentionally disruptive leaders to maintain an organization's focus while pursuing transformative change?

- How can intentionally disruptive leaders manage their boards, shareholders, teammates, and other stakeholders throughout the different phases of intentionally disruptive organizational transformation?

- What strategies can intentionally disruptive leaders use to manage personal and family dislocations?

- What role do core values play in being an intentionally disruptive leader?

In the current business climate, success isn't only about surviving a constant stream of disruptions; it's about actively and intentionally disrupting the status quo in a thoughtful way. Whether or not you consider yourself an intentionally disruptive leader, it is a valuable strategy. Regardless of the type of leader you are or the type of group you lead, all leaders need some elements of disruptive leadership. If you're going to be a leader, you have to deal with disruption, manage risks, keep your people motivated, maintain your core values, and make difficult decisions. It's not an easy task, and it's not for the faint of heart.

No matter what leadership role you hold or aspire to hold, this book offers viable strategies for dealing with difficult circumstances. You may not currently embody the elements that make a leader an intentional disrupter, but this book will demonstrate key components you can incorporate that will aid you on your path toward successful leadership. Furthermore, this book will give you tips and tools for surviving disruption in your environment and strategies for how to deploy intentionally disruptive techniques in your professional and personal lives.

This is not a technical business book; it's an emotional leadership survival guide that speaks to the trend in emerging leaders to be connected to a mission rather than just a salary. This book was written for today's leaders and the emerging leaders of tomorrow. You may be an athlete or team captain of your high school or college sport, you may be an emerging or aspiring leader of your own business or large organization, or you may be a CEO facing incredibly difficult challenges. No matter what situation you find yourself in, this book demonstrates that taking thoughtful risks is a powerful leadership strategy. These are my life lessons—hard-fought and hard-earned—from the baseball field to the boardroom.

Having survived disruptive environments in my personal and professional lives, I know there are disturbances for which you cannot prepare. You can, however, plan to be disrupted; you can acclimate yourself to chaos so that you can stay calm in its midst. Though I didn't realize it in my early youth, I was preparing myself daily through baseball training to survive what has evolved into a career made out of disruptions—some led by myself and others led by outside forces. Throughout this book, we will look at how disruptions have the power to control us unless we develop the skills and tools needed to control them. Gaining an early understanding of how to survive disruptions proved to be invaluable when I entered the challenging field of healthcare. Learning to harness the power of disruption and use it in an intentional way became the key to my success in business.

PART I

CLEARING THE PATH FOR INTENTIONAL DISRUPTION

CHAPTER 1

HEALTHCARE: THE NEW WILD WEST

THE MORNING AFTER the 2018 midterm election, I turned on the television to hear the results. I learned that several races were too close to call, so I flipped between all the cable networks to discern the "middle ground" of what the results (or lack thereof) might mean for the future. I found that each network had surmised, based on polling of their target audiences, what the top three concerns were for American voters heading into the polls. The answers differed, but one showed up first on each network's list: healthcare. It isn't often that all cable networks agree on anything, but this much was true—healthcare was on everyone's mind.

For someone who had chosen healthcare as a profession, I wasn't sure whether the public's priority was a good thing or a bad thing. On the one hand, I passionately believe that what I do every day makes a huge difference in people's lives by marshaling every resource at my disposal to provide care to people who need it—especially the type of care Kindred provides to critically ill people. On the other hand, there are so many challenges in the healthcare system that we all face, and the public's interest reflects to a significant extent frustration with what isn't currently working, and that is a responsibility that those of us working every day in this field take very seriously.

To understand how to use intentional disruption as a business strategy, you have to understand some basic facts and context about a very complex topic—healthcare and aging care in America.

CURRENT STATE OF AFFAIRS IN HEALTHCARE

When I'm at cocktail parties, I like to ask the group, "How many of you have had a sick loved one—child, parent, grandparent, friend—who you have tried to help navigate through the healthcare delivery system?" Each time, at least 80 percent of the room raises their hands. It always amazes me how many people, besides the patients themselves, are affected by the healthcare system. Despite the divisions among Americans, one of the things that unites us is that we all encounter challenges within the healthcare system. Even for sophisticated professionals in the field, healthcare can be complex and unpredictable. Understanding the causes that led to these current challenges can help consumers better understand how to seek the care they need for themselves and their loved ones.

WHAT YOU NEED TO KNOW ABOUT HEALTHCARE

- Everything about the way we consume and utilize healthcare is changing rapidly.

- The Affordable Care Act helped shine a light on the costs of and access to healthcare.

- Consumerism is driving more decisions than ever in healthcare.

- Baby boomers are becoming Medicare eligible at a rapidly escalating pace.

- Anxieties are growing over the future of access, cost, and care.

- The COVID-19 pandemic has placed even more focus on the social and racial disparities of our current healthcare delivery system.

When I entered the healthcare field, I did not realize it was the Wild West of industries. Healthcare is incredibly complex and is often a challenging field to navigate. The first thing to know about healthcare is that it is changing rapidly. Even for insiders, it is difficult to keep up with the fast-paced, daily fluctuations.

Healthcare is disruptive. There are several factors that have led to this increasingly chaotic system, and we will discuss each fully in this chapter:

- **Rapid change.** One of the reasons more people are aware of healthcare issues is that more people are affected by them, as evidenced by my informal cocktail party polls. Ever since the inception of the Affordable Care Act (ACA), or Obamacare, in 2010, there has been massive media coverage of the industry. The ACA was meant to simplify certain aspects of the health-care system. Instead, it was a match that lit a fire that has fueled political and ideological debates about healthcare ever since. Since the ACA was signed into law at the height of social media use, it became a viral discussion. This public awareness, coupled with a growing surge in technology, has created an environment rife with challenges for consumers and for people in the business. It is a constantly disrupted environment for anyone who touches the healthcare system, which is nearly every citizen.

- **Consumerism.** Consumerism is a driving force in American culture, and healthcare is no exception. Because of the digitization of America, we can buy everything online, from paper towels to DNA testing. We can also compare prices online. Consumers can discover how to get the cheapest hip replacement, for example. Access to information has motivated consumers to be their own health advocates, as evidenced by the popularity of search engines and WebMD. The ACA also transferred more of the financial burden to consumers with the inception of higher deductibles, larger copays, and a shift from employer-sponsored costs to employee-sponsored costs. With this growing interest and investment in the healthcare sphere, more people are cognizant that healthcare is expensive and that the system is in need of repair.

- **Demographics.** American demographics are shifting quickly as baby boomers turn sixty-five and become Medicare eligible. Many people describe it as a great silver tsunami coming over our country. Seniors will require more healthcare, utilize more resources, and cost more money to the system. With these new challenges come new questions about how prepared we are and how resilient our government systems are. Due to the growing number of seniors and easy access to the internet, more people are aware of and concerned by the rapidly changing industry. The American public is asking regulators, policy makers, and business insiders, "As we get older, how much care are we entitled to? How much is that care going to cost? Who is going to pay? And who's going to take care of us?" These are profound questions that directly affect the lives of every American, regardless of age, race, health, or gender.

- **Healthcare disparities.** During 2020, Americans of every age and every demographic saw the growing disparities in our healthcare delivery system as we faced the global COVID-19 pandemic. Healthcare was no longer something people took for granted. Each day, as COVID-19 spread, every American was forced to think about the suddenness of what getting the virus might mean, of how it could affect them individually or as a community, and of what resources were available in an increasingly complicated healthcare delivery system. Our lives were collectively disrupted by the crisis, and our focus on healthcare and its many disparities in our society was also suddenly thrust into focus.

Medicare Facts

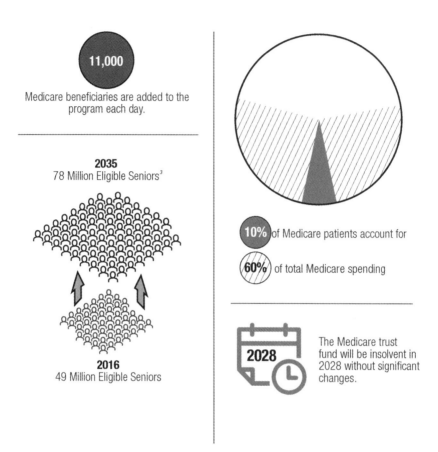

11,000

Medicare beneficiaries are added to the program each day.

2035
78 Million Eligible Seniors[3]

2016
49 Million Eligible Seniors

10% of Medicare patients account for

60% of total Medicare spending

2028 The Medicare trust fund will be insolvent in 2028 without significant changes.

What we've learned at Kindred Healthcare is that the emerging aging tsunami will not just affect the seventy-eight million American seniors; it will likely affect their adult children as well—in fact, it will affect their female children most. This creates an entire generation of adults who are attempting to care for their own young children's needs at the same time as they're addressing the requirements of their aging parents. Today a middle-aged parent might worry about paying for

---

3   Jonathan Vespa, "The Graying of America: More Adults than Kids by 2035," US Census Bureau, last modified October 8, 2019, https://www.census.gov/library/stories/2018/03/grayingamerica.html.

their child's vaccinations and medications and concurrently be navigating a challenging system on behalf of their aging parent(s). This is an enormous burden to bear, and we don't yet know what societal implications this might have on our culture.

Together, these factors combine to create a milieu that is incredibly difficult for everyone involved. Inarguably, our healthcare model

> What I have learned in my life—behind the plate and in the boardroom—is that with the right strategies you can survive a disruptive environment.

has been disrupted by these challenges. What I have learned in my life—behind the plate and in the boardroom—is that with the right strategies you can survive a disruptive environment. By providing the tools I have cultivated as president and chief executive officer at Kindred Healthcare, I hope to make the system more manageable for health consumers and their families and provide support and resources to ease the burden for an entire generation of Americans.

WHAT IS "POST-ACUTE" CARE, AND HOW DOES IT FIT INTO THE HEALTHCARE SYSTEM?

Whether your community is big or small, urban or rural, you know where to go when you have medical needs. If you have a baby, you go to the maternity ward at the hospital or birth center. If you have a non-life-threatening issue, you go to your doctor or an urgent treatment clinic. If you are in need of emergency care, you go to the emergency room. In these situations, called "acute care," it is clear where to seek help.

But what happens after you've been discharged from the hospital but are still in need of care? What do you do as the patient, the consumer, the payor when you are in need of care after you leave the hospital? This is known as "post-acute care," or care received after the care in a community hospital is complete.

Not long ago, as the supposed "healthcare expert" in the family, I received a hurried call from my father about his ninety-seven-year-old mother: "Your grandmother fell in the shower and broke her neck! What should I do?" I quickly responded, "Call 911!" He explained that she had been taken to the emergency room, checked into a bed, and stabilized. The doctors decided that at her advanced age, she was not a candidate for surgery. They did recognize, however, that she would require further care, but she was not going to get it from the hospital. My father called me because he didn't know where to go from there. This is where Kindred Healthcare becomes an invaluable resource. Ultimately, we found her an "inpatient rehabilitation facility"—a specialty hospital focused on intensive rehabilitation care—where she received care for several weeks. Now, at one hundred one years old, she is as spry as she was before the accident and still travels to Louisville, Kentucky, to visit her three great-granddaughters.

The post-acute sector by facility type is organized into five components:

- Long-term acute care hospital (LTAC)
- Inpatient rehabilitation facility (IRF)
- Skilled nursing facility (SNF)
- Home health
- Hospice care

A **long-term acute care hospital (LTAC)** is similar to what a regular acute care hospital looks like, but to be eligible to stay in an LTAC, one must stay 25 days or more. For comparison, the average regular hospital stay is 3.8 days. In order to qualify for care in an LTAC, a patient must be quite sick and require an extended stay. They also usually have multiple comorbidities, or multiple conditions of illness, which might include compromised respiratory system, kidneys, or nutritional status. These issues need to be resolved before they can move home or to another level of care.

An **inpatient rehabilitation facility (IRF)** is a step down from an LTAC. These patients may have suffered strokes, brain injuries, or spinal cord injuries. Like my grandmother, these are patients who need extended rehabilitation care following an accident or injury. For this reason, to qualify to be in an IRF, you must be able to sustain, at least on average, three hours of rehabilitation daily. These facilities have massive rehab gyms and teams of speech, occupational, and physical therapists.

A **skilled nursing facility (SNF)** is much more commonly known by most Americans. An SNF is a nursing center for somebody who is able to leave the hospital but is unable to return home. These patients need extended stays and may be there for a multitude of reasons. They might have a rehabilitative issue, but more commonly today, they have degenerative brain diseases like Alzheimer's or dementia.

Home health allows the patient to stay at home with frequent visits from nurses and/or therapists. It's a Medicare benefit that is popular with many Americans able to care for themselves with minimal intervention.

Hospice care is end-of-life care administered at home. This service provides comfort and compassion for many individuals. As I have witnessed within my own family, hospice care is both tremendously cost effective and consumer friendly.

For the seventy-eight million seniors eligible for Medicare by 2035, these post-acute care settings will be vital, since there will be an entire generation of Americans navigating the system. But this brief summary doesn't answer questions that individuals, families, payors, and policy makers have about these vital services. Will they be like my father and not know what to do when the hospital releases their family members? Which post-acute setting is the most appropriate for seniors leaving a hospital? For what period of time? How much will it cost? How much should it cost? That's where Kindred comes in. It is our goal and mission at Kindred to be the provider that can help individuals find the care they require and deserve in efficient and compassionate ways. In a nutshell, it's finding the right care at the right place, at the right price.

KINDRED'S ROLE AS "INTEGRATED" POST-ACUTE CARE PROVIDER

At our peak, Kindred Healthcare was the largest diversified provider of post-acute care in the country. Kindred has been the largest LTAC provider in the country, one of the largest IRF providers, the largest SNF provider, the largest home health provider, and one of the largest hospice providers. This didn't happen overnight. We set out to be a fully diversified provider of post-acute services to create a seamless continuum of care, expressly to solve the challenges noted above—and we did this through a series of aggressive acquisitions and organic growth. Kindred offers the benefit of broad continuum of post-acute care under one company.

Kindred Healthcare's Peak at a Glance

47 States

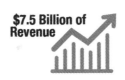
$7.5 Billion of Revenue

115,000 Employees

53rd largest non-government employer in the country

383 on the Fortune 500 list, publicly traded on the New York Stock Exchange, NYSE:KND.

In 2017, we had more than one million patients come through Kindred's doors. If you add our employees, their dependents, and our patients, we essentially touched two million lives—either with care, benefits, or salary. We are a significant part of the U.S. healthcare economy and the economy at large. We are dedicated to promoting healing, providing hope, and preserving the dignity of all the families we have the honor to work with.

Just as consumers have questions about where to send their loved ones, regulators have questions about which patients are appropriate for which types of care. At Kindred, we hope to simplify the process of finding and accessing the care that patients need. As we've established, the healthcare industry is a disrupted and challenging one for consumers and providers alike.

Kindred Healthcare Timeline

The Rise and Fall of Vencor

Rebranding, Right Sizing and Preparing for Growth

Focus, Innovation and Intentional Disruption

1

1985

Vencor Founded

1995

Vencor purchases Hillhaven with 300+SNFs

1998

△ VENTAS®

Real estate split off to form Ventas

1999

Vencor files for bankruptcy

2

2001

Rebranded as Kindred Healthcare in April, joined the NYSE as KND in May

2003

Florida SNF Divestiture

2007

PharMerica®

Simultaneously spun off and merged our pharmacy business with PharMerica

2007

Made our first home health and hospice acquisitions

3

2011

Acquired RehabCare

2013

Began SNF Divestiture

2015

Acquired Centerre

2015

Acquired Gentiva, becoming the largest Home Health and Hospice Provider

2017

Completed SNF Divestiture

2019

Completed the process of going private via acquisition and splitting off of our Home Health business with three partners, TPG, Welsh Carson, and Humana

THE EVOLUTION OF KINDRED

Though the name of the company has changed over the years, from Vencor, when the company was first founded in 1983, to Kindred Healthcare, the mission of the company has remained the same from its inception: Kindred was built to provide a range of care services for aging America and to address the needs of elderly patients who leave the hospital and need more care.

THE RISE AND FALL OF VENCOR

Vencor was founded in 1985 by Bruce Lunsford and Mike Barr, two thoughtful healthcare entrepreneurs who sought to build a post-acute facility business. They started with two LTAC hospitals and eventually grew Vencor into one of the largest LTAC companies in the country. In 1995, they acquired Hillhaven, one of the largest nursing center operators at the time. With this acquisition, Vencor tripled in size, took on a significant amount of debt, and became the largest nursing home operator in the country.

In 1997, the Balanced Budget Act was passed under the Clinton administration. This agreement virtually decimated the nursing center industry. With one stroke of a pen, Vencor, which had grown exponentially by this time, was in danger. Just as this major reimbursement change was occurring, Lunsford and Barr devised an idea to split the company into an operating company and a real estate company. At the time, this was a revolutionary strategy, though later it would become a more common strategic move in healthcare. Vencor became the operating company, and a new company was created called Ventas, which would become the landlord and owner of all of the real estate assets of the company. Ventas has since become one of the biggest real estate investment trusts in the country, with roughly a $30 billion market capitalization today. Vencor, on the other hand, found itself in worsening financial trouble and had to file for bankruptcy in 1999.

REBRANDING, RESIZING, AND CREATING A CULTURE OF QUALITY AND COMPLIANCE

In 2001, Vencor emerged from bankruptcy and was renamed Kindred Healthcare. It was relisted on the New York Stock Exchange under the ticker KND. Over the next decade, Kindred sought to create a culture of quality and compliance that reestablished its strategic place in the post-acute continuum. The focus was to create a platform to address the broader issues of post-acute care.

CREATING A PLATFORM FOR GROWTH

From 2010 to 2017, Kindred focused on creating a platform for growth. We will discuss additional details in future chapters, but during this time the company embarked upon a methodical but aggressive growth plan to expand the scope of post-acute services to create a continuum of care for patients and families. We also "divested" a number of assets, such as SNFs, to address reimbursement changes. During this time, we acquired a number of competitors, including RehabCare (outpatient and SNF-based rehab), Gentiva, and Centerre (inpatient hospital rehab), which positioned Kindred to grow and transform the post-acute care industry. In December 2017, our board announced a transaction that created two separate, privately held companies in addition to refinancing our balance sheet, fixing our financial structure, and, ultimately, establishing a foundation that we can build on for the next ten years.

MY RISE THROUGH KINDRED

In 2005, I was thirty-four years old, living in Scottsdale, Arizona, with my wife, Shelly. We had recently been discussing what, if any, next steps I should take with my career. The prospect of a new adventure excited us both, and we were eager to explore opportunities. Around this time, I was contacted by Paul Diaz, who was then CEO at Kindred. He wanted to recruit me as his potential successor, starting with the job of president of the Rehab Division, the smallest of the four businesses Kindred held at the time.

Upon learning more about the company, I was immediately intrigued by Kindred's dedication to its mission and values. The entire team was passionate about taking care of those who couldn't care for themselves. In my interviews, Eddie Kuntz, the executive board chair—my predecessor's predecessor—revealed that I wasn't joining only to be the president of the smallest of four divisions; rather, there would be an opportunity, though not certain or guaranteed, to progress through the organization and ultimately take the helm as CEO. For a guy in his mid-thirties, this was an appealing but intimidating opportunity.

I can't say that my wife was thrilled about the disruption this created for our family plans (more on that in chapter 9), but she could understand why I was interested in the company, and she understood why I would want to be a part of a team that provided quality health services to aging Americans. After many discussions, we made the decision to move our growing family to Louisville, Kentucky.

During my tenure at Kindred Healthcare, I have served as president of the Rehabilitation Division (2005–08), as president of the Hospital Division (2008–10), as chief operating officer of Kindred (2010–12), and finally as president and chief executive officer. I led the acquisition of the publicly traded healthcare company Gentiva, the largest operator of home care and hospice. We also divested businesses that were poor fits, totaling more than $3 billion in revenue.

Serving at multiple levels and in various divisions at Kindred prior to my appointment as CEO gave me two primary advantages over an external appointee. First, it enabled me to become a content expert. I knew all the businesses we ran, which enabled me to deal with complicated issues quickly and decisively and in turn be a better leader. Second, having experience running three of our divisions also fostered an empathetic leadership style that greatly benefited our team members, especially our clinicians. I had seen their hard work and dedication, and I admired our team camaraderie.

When I think about my desire to help others navigate complicated systems like healthcare, I am reminded of my mother. Raised in the Bronx, my mom assumed that if you could survive New York City in your youth, then you could survive anything. She believed this so strongly, in fact, that she and I took many weekend trips to New York City in which she essentially turned me loose. She would hand me cash or a credit card at the start of the trip, and it was my job to hail cabs, make reservations, book theater tickets, and pay bills. "If you can navigate this," she'd say, "you can navigate anything." I'm not sure I was aware at the time, but her desire to teach me to stay calm amid chaos has proven an invaluable asset in my career in the healthcare industry.

Not unlike my years spent as a baseball catcher in the hot Florida sun, I have observed the healthcare playing field from every angle. Despite the chaotic nature of the healthcare industry, I've always believed that if I can call the pitches, set the defenses, and rally the troops, I can help our millions of customers survive the disrupted system that confounds them today but might care for them tomorrow.

LESSONS FROM THE FIELD

- Challenge yourself with the unfamiliar.

- Observe the whole field before calling the play.

- Be ready to learn.

- Prepare yourself for the unpredictable.

- Stay calm between the lines.

- Plan to be disrupted.

CHAPTER 2

RALLYING THE TEAM

Midway through 2015—having been the CEO of Kindred Healthcare for only a few months—my general counsel came into my office to inform me that the three-year investigation we had been under by the Department of Justice (DOJ) and the U.S. Attorney's Office had taken a turn for the worse. Years earlier, the DOJ had filed a lawsuit against a subsidiary of ours, RehabCare, accusing them of overinflating billing for services in their contract rehabilitation business. This case involved actions taken by RehabCare before we acquired the company in 2011, but we were nonetheless being held responsible. When you acquire a company in a stock deal, you acquire all the liabilities that come with it.

When I met with my general counsel and chief financial officer to discuss the status of the investigation, my general counsel cut right to the chase: "We've exhausted virtually every avenue and path that we can play out with the government. They've thrown an enormous amount of resources against us, and if we don't settle, they're threatening to take this to a jury trial. It will be difficult and costly to defend, and the outcome is uncertain." She had clearly already thought the jury process out, and it was rife with problems. First, in our current corporate litigation climate, juries often view big corporate entities like Kindred as malicious before the case is even tried. Second, there was no question that the field was weighted far to the advantage of the government. It's not just a question of losing due to unsafe liability. Because the government can double or triple the damages a jury awards and then add statutory penalties on top, whatever you're liable for in a jury trial can actually turn out to be ten times worse!

> For a guy who likes to play offense and to cause disruption as a tool for business growth and success, I was now faced with an external threat–the all-powerful government–disrupting my world.

My general counsel and CFO estimated that if this went to trial and we lost, we could wind up paying the plaintiffs and the government around $2 billion. If their calculations were correct, the company would have to file for Chapter 11 protection, potentially putting us out of business. For a guy who likes to play offense and to cause disruption as a tool for business growth and success, I was now faced with an external threat—the all-powerful government—disrupting my world. This was proving to be a harsh start to my rookie year as a CEO.

I asked my advisors what the settlement might look like. They made it clear that if we were willing to write a check for $125 million, we could potentially put the case to rest without admitting any guilt or wrongdoing. This way we could proceed with our business affairs—or what would be left of them—and avoid a protracted jury trial. On the other hand, my CFO reminded me that while going to court certainly wasn't a compelling option, $125 million was the equivalent of one full year's cash flow generation for the entire company. He said that while I might want to settle so as not to face the stiffer penalties, I should understand the repercussions for the company if I used all of our cash for the year. To make matters worse, this settlement would be due on January 1, 2016. If we took the settlement, I'd essentially be using all the cash proceeds for the company for the entire year on the first day of the new year. If there had been any honeymoon period for my new position as CEO, it was certainly over. I was three months in, and it was time to lead.

TIME TO PLAY OFFENSE

After my general counsel and CFO informed me about the investigation and our available options, I remember thinking, "I've only been the CEO for three months! This is totally disrupting my plans for this company." I had ideas about where I wanted to deploy capital, where I wanted to grow, how I wanted to be perceived. This disruption certainly wasn't a part of those plans. I had to absorb all of the information and devise what my path forward would be.

I remember saying to my advisors, "I just don't understand how it has come to this. We've been providing care and value to these people all of these years." My lawyer responded, "That's true, but the government doesn't see it that way." I knew there was a lot of work ahead of me. I would need to get my board up to speed, get my shareholders prepared, get my employees and teammates equipped, and get my creditors and bankers ready for what eventually could be a substantial cash payment made to the government.

I thought over all the scenarios overnight, and by morning, I had a plan. I decided the best action would be to play offense: we would settle, fix, communicate, and push forward. The board knew we had been under investigation, but the gravity of the settlement was certainly going to be hard for them to hear. I called the chairwoman of my board and explained that I would recommend to the board that we settle with the government and pay the $125 million. It was important in my new stewardship of the company to put this behind us, and we could not risk the broader potential consequences that could result from going to trial. As painful as the settlement was going to be, I felt the uncertainty of the case was affecting our business. For this reason, I had decided to be aggressive in resolving the issue.

Even with my plan in place, it was still a challenge to execute. Our financial leaders had to figure out where we were going to find $125 million. We had a significant amount of debt at the time. I knew that a large one-time payment like this was going to make our bondholders nervous, so I had to work with them to ease their worries. We also had to begin preparing our shareholders that we were planning to take this $125 million reserve against earnings. I needed to internally prepare how to communicate the news to my 115,000 teammates. We were not admitting wrongdoing; nor were we blaming anybody for what happened—this was an unfortunate by-product of acquiring another company years prior.

It was important to the entire team that the mission, values, and culture of our company remained strong during this time. The biggest issue a public company faces is uncertainty. I knew if we stayed committed to our core values and communicated appropriately with our team, the circumstances might be viewed more positively than negatively. In many ways, stocks and equity values can rally around an indeterminate situation if the plan of action is certain and transparent. If we could tell the story the right way to our shareholders, bondholders, and employees, then we might be able to turn this around. Over the course of the next twelve weeks, with my personal core values and the mission of Kindred as my guides, I rallied the troops around this plan.

My board was extremely supportive and approved the settlement. They agreed that it was best for the company to put this issue behind us. We issued a press release announcing the settlement with the government on January 12, 2016. I spoke to our shareholders and our bondholders directly. Although they all seemed concerned, they also appreciated the level of transparency I was providing. After the announcement, our stock price went up, not down.

Creating the same transparency with our employee base was somewhat more complicated because we have a large, diverse workforce spread out across the country. We drafted at least five direct communications from me to all of our teammates. These have since evolved into a quarterly staff newsletter called *Touching Base*, which we publish digitally and on social media to ensure it is accessible to our entire team. We also held and broadcasted town halls that allowed team members to ask me questions directly by phone, videoconferencing, or in person. We established cascade communication tiers and talking points, ensuring teammates heard from their managers as well. Finally, because many of our teammates, like our nursing staff, have limited time for office communications, we created an app called Kindred for Me. To date, forty-eight thousand employees use this app to stay abreast of company issues and communications when it is convenient for their schedule.

Having communicated transparently and taken such decisive action to get the issue resolved, I was able to garner significant amounts of goodwill with our employee base. While it was a painful experience, we ultimately came out of it with a more solid foundation than we had before. Though it wasn't the easy transition I had hoped for as a novice CEO, it gave me strategies for dealing with disruptions that would soon prove more valuable than I could have known.

LESSONS FOR RALLYING YOUR TEAM

- Be ready to lead. Teammates and coworkers want confidence plus decisiveness in their CEO during tough decisions.

- Have a plan for executing your decisions.

- Be aggressive.

- Establish transparency with your team.

- Be available to your team.

CHAPTER 3

SURPRISE! YOU'RE ON CNN

*"What do you mean Sean Hannity wants me on his show
to talk about why Kindred doesn't support the American flag?"*

*"Well, Fox and CNN have been telling its viewers all afternoon
that our company doesn't support a military mother putting an
American flag on her office wall."*

*"Susan, you can't just come into my office and tell me,
'Surprise, you're on CNN!'"*

IN ALL MY YEARS of training to be a healthcare executive, I was
not prepared for the digital and social media disruption I encountered
in 2009. As a leader, especially in healthcare, you will sometimes face
incredibly disruptive events that can threaten the core of the organization's existence. Even though you cannot prepare for the specifics
of a disruption, you can prepare for the disruption itself using the
lessons I've learned. The "flag crisis," as it became known, was a type
of disruption I had never even imagined.

On May 15, 2009, a hospital nurse supervisor in one of our Texas
facilities hung an American flag in the cubicle she shared with four
other Kindred employees. Several days later, her manager approached
her and told her that some individuals in the hospital found the size

of the flag "offensive." As a result, one of four employees who shared the cubicle with the nurse supervisor removed the flag from the wall, rolled it up, and placed it in the corner. The nurse supervisor who owned the flag found it rolled up in the corner and approached the hospital's senior management team. She said it was unfair that her three-foot-by-five-foot flag had been deemed too big and thus offensive. The CEO of the facility told the flag owner that there was in fact a flag outside the facility, and as a result, her cubicle flag need not be in the work area. The employee, feeling unheard, reached out to a local news station, which ran the story, including her comment "I find it very frightening because if I can't display my flag, what other freedoms will I lose before all is said and done?"

I imagine the outrage if something like this happened as I'm writing this in 2020. Social media would go absolutely nuts! People on one side would say Kindred hated America, while people on the other side would say we should not only take the flag down, we should burn it. All of this would play out on Twitter and Facebook. You can only imagine the toxicity of the comments and replies.

Well, this was 2009, more than a decade ago, and we were all just beginning to come to grips with the disruption that social media would create in our lives. Despite living in a pre-Trump, pre-COVID-19 world, tensions in our country were already growing, and social media platforms had become the match that was about to light a huge bonfire!

After the piece aired, Fox News and CNN picked it up. In total, the event generated hundreds of television stories, including on most of the large cable networks across the country. There was also a series of radio segments and newspaper articles. By the time Sean Hannity covered the story, it had gone viral and was being shared across social media.

DIGITAL DISRUPTION

Because many of Kindred's facilities operate under the Kindred name, any negative story, whether healthcare related or not, is bad for the brand. In 2009, social media was a revolutionary new tool used by consumers, and the story could be disseminated faster than we could respond. Kindred, like most companies in 2009, had not yet recognized the speed and ferocity of the social media age. Today, we have become numb to even a presidential tweet, but in 2009, most of us didn't realize how quickly the world was changing around us. Internet coverage was widespread and perhaps the most influential medium for amplifying and spreading the controversy. Discussions through blogs, Twitter, Facebook, YouTube, and other social networking websites intensified throughout the crisis. Kindred received thousands of complaint emails. Because this was before social media was being used regularly by corporate America, Kindred had to respond to each email, phone call, and letter. We quickly realized that social media had changed the way people communicate—and if used well, it held for us the potential to speak directly with consumers.

Only a year or so earlier, I had attended a healthcare conference where there was much talk about the burgeoning field of social media. When I returned, I went straight to my head of Marketing and Communications: "Susan, what is this thing I've been hearing about called Facebook? Do we need to be doing anything about this?" Susan gathered some experts—including one of the two people in the country with a PhD in social media at the time—to help us understand these new platforms. Not long after this presentation, before we had even set up our own Kindred Facebook page, the flag incident went viral.

SERVICE RECOVERY STRATEGY

David Teece, a professor at the University of California, Berkeley, orig-
inated the theory of "dynamic capabilities" to explain how companies
must be stable enough to deliver products and services and also remain
robust and resilient enough to adapt to fluctuating circumstances. He
put forth three types of managerial activities that make a capability
dynamic: *sensing*, which means identifying and assessing opportunities outside your company; *seizing*, which means mobilizing your
resources to capture value from those opportunities; and *reconfiguring*,
which denotes continuous renewal. Teece posited that

> *enterprises must employ sensing, seizing, and reconfiguring
> mechanisms to direct their financial resources consistent with
> marketplace needs and imperatives. However, as a matter of
> pure theory, enterprises need not continuously reinvent themselves.
> The need to reinvent depends on events, anticipated or otherwise.
> If the ecosystem in which the enterprise is embedded remains
> stable, the need to change can be modulated accordingly.
> Indeed, if an enterprise controls standards, or can somehow help
> stabilize its own environment, then it may not need to engage in
> the continuous and costly exploration of radical alternatives.* [4]

As Teece's theory demonstrates, when ecosystems shift, no matter
the cause, a dynamic leader must respond accordingly. With the advent
of social media, the landscape had certainly shifted. Even though this
was a major disruption that we could not have predicted, we had to
respond to it. We had already begun to educate ourselves about these
revolutionary new communication platforms, but considering the

---

4   David J. Teece, "Explicating Dynamic Capabilities: The Nature and Microfoundations
     of (Sustainable) Enterprise Performance," *Strategic Management Journal* 28 (August
     2007): 1319–50, https://doi.org/10.1002/smj.640.

recent bad press, we had to do more. I asked my head of Marketing and Communications what we could do to ensure it didn't happen again and protect the company. We needed to become best in class at dealing with crisis management, service recovery, and brand building. This led to the formation of an entire social media and brand management strategy and made us an innovator in the healthcare digital field.

An organization has constant external pressures about resource allocation. At a time when marketing budgets were tight and companies weren't spending money this way, I made the decision to invest in protecting the goodwill of our brand. We deployed significant capital to build a brand and service recovery model, including the creation of a new Social and Reputation Department with many full-time team members. The company now invests millions of dollars annually in these programs. We also made certain that we were attending conferences and continually educating ourselves about social media and digital platforms.

We realized when the flag incident happened in 2009 that consumers did not have a means to channel all of their angst against the company, so it went viral. Now that we have social media and other digital platforms, the company can manage disruptions before they circulate. Today we have six hundred Facebook pages. We have landing pages for every single property that we own. We have 3,500 YouTube videos, and we are consistently sharing information about our brand and our business. We also use Reputation.com—an aggregator of over thirty social media sites—to alert us when reviews are posted online. Now we have a team in place all day, every day that receives and responds to reviewers within two hours. Due to the team's hard work, we now generate approximately eight hundred reviews a month, with less than 6 percent of those being negative.

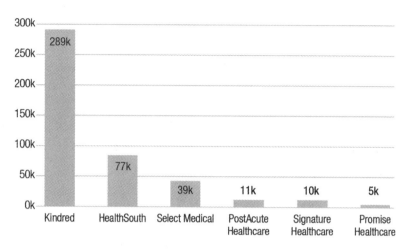

Kindred Share of Voice Across Social Media 2018
(Likes, Comments, Posts and other Key Metrics)

We now have a top-level social media program. According to TrackMaven, which measures Kindred against competitors in the social media space, we are 300 percent higher in terms of our reputation than any of our competitors. Because of the breadth of our digital and social media operation, we are the only post-acute care provider that is asked to speak at healthcare conferences to discuss what we've implemented and how we've done it.

Building a Reputation Through Innovation Investment

Kindred's State-by-State Reputation Before and After an Aggressive Investment in Online Reputation Management

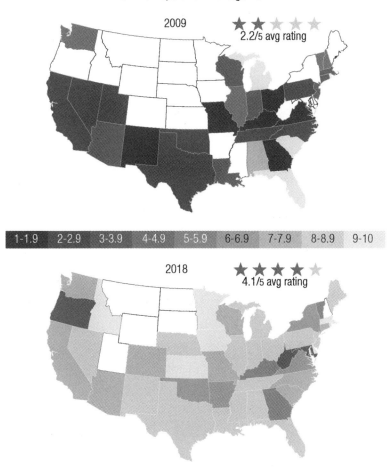

In addition to the digital and social media response strategies, Kindred's security was a big concern after the flag incident. We first needed to ensure that our team was safe. This wasn't easy in an ever-changing atmosphere of divisive social commentary. Some of the Kindred teammates who were named in the story, including myself and my family, received death threats after the story aired. We decided to reimagine the security of our corporate campus, where we have about 1,200 full-time employees working in a large urban market. We also hired security guards and installed security systems in each of our thousands of locations across the country.

In 2009, viral disruptions like the flag incident were totally new to corporate enterprise. It may seem routine to deal with disruptions like these now, but at the time, responding to the flag incident in a burgeoning digital environment required swift, decisive action. Though I could not have prepared myself for the specifics of this disturbance, I was prepared for external disruptions that would test me as a leader and call upon the intentional disruption strategies I had been developing since my youth.

> You can't plan on the nature of the disruption, but you can plan for the disruption itself.

SURVIVING UNFORESEEN DISRUPTIONS

I learned years ago on the baseball field that a catcher has to consider the entire playing field. I had to find a way to keep all options available as I considered the fluid and changing strategy of each game. I try to approach business situations with this same tactic. A company is built on moving parts and fluid players, and I try to consider all of these pieces when developing strategy and making decisions. Regardless of preparation and perspective, however, there *will* be external disruptions that you never see coming. You can't plan on the nature of the disruption, but you can plan for the disruption itself.

Ideally, as a leader, you want to be proactive, but the reality is that there will be circumstances in which you will have to be reactive. You can't prepare for everything. When these disruptions occur, you have to try to remain calm, as much for your team as for your own sanity. This mindfulness also allows you not to react immediately. In times of stress, you have to remind yourself that you have time to ask the necessary questions and talk to the people on the team. This can help a leader triangulate what's happening on the ground. After I obtain the facts as best I can, I always try to develop a game plan or a series of actions that I *might* take. Before actually taking them, however, I talk to the content experts, who usually know more about the situational tactic than I do. In the flag case, I talked to experts in crisis management, brand management, and the digital world.

I remember reaching out to Jonathan Blum, one of my board members during this time, who had served as the head of communications for Yum! Brands. This was a large public company that owned Taco Bell, Kentucky Fried Chicken (KFC), and Pizza Hut. A few weeks prior to the flag incident, KFC had launched a new grilled chicken product on *The Oprah Winfrey Show*. The promotion went awry and backfired because KFC wasn't prepared for the demand. The story, you may recall, went viral. Jonathan walked me through their strategy, which included sending the president of KFC back on Oprah's show to apologize. I remember him telling me that however I proceeded with Kindred's recovery strategy, don't end up on *Oprah*: "CNN's one thing; *Oprah*'s another."

Once you have spoken with trusted experts on how to proceed, develop your own action plan. Before enacting it, however, you have to empower your team to deal with the issues according to the plan you've agreed to. As a leader, there's no way you can be everywhere; nor should you be doing everything. Ultimately, to recover from unforeseen disruptions, you have to trust the team around you and empower them to execute the plan. In circumstances like these, there is a directive role for the leader, but ultimately, the plan must be executed by the team.

When the team has been educated and empowered, it's time to enact the plan. In dealing with disruption, your strategy is as much about *how* you execute the plan as it is the plan itself: put the plan into effect with every ounce of energy, urgency, and force you can muster. You include every resource you have, and you essentially go to battle. Have confidence in your instincts and intellect. Think less about the battle and more about the outcome you desire. Oftentimes the best way to tackle disruption is to attack without fear.

Experience and preparation create enormous amounts of confidence, and that's why I am so dedicated to both. Kindred's flag incident was unforeseen and unpredictable. Having happened once, however, it's now more understandable. With effective leadership and action plans, even the unanticipated disruptions can become more manageable.

There was certainly a defensive aspect to our service recovery tactics to ensure that the same level of disruption didn't reoccur. What started as a reactive way to intervene and manage events that come at us in real time has evolved into a proactive, offensive strategy to advance the business. We still have employee conflict within our system, but what we put in place ten years ago has protected us and served us well because we are able to manage the unforeseen disruptions that lie ahead in our inherently disruptive digital world.

LESSONS FOR SURVIVING UNFORESEEN DISRUPTIONS

- Remain calm. Keep emotions in check.

- Obtain all the facts before launching into a response.

- Develop an action plan; don't just shoot first and aim later.

- Review with experts.

- Empower the team.

- As you put your plan into action, trust your process and focus on the end result.

PART II

LEADING WITH INTENTIONAL DISRUPTION

CHAPTER 4

ADVANCING DISRUPTIVE LEADERSHIP IN A PUBLIC COMPANY

IN 2012, WHEN I WAS still chief operating officer of Kindred, I attended a leadership meeting in Austin, Texas, with my predecessor, Kindred's then CEO, Paul Diaz. On our flight together, we discussed the future of the company. We talked about the home health industry and where it fit into the healthcare ecosystem. I wondered aloud if it was something we could figure out. He looked at me and offered, "I think you should try. I think you should build a home health business." I replied, "You want *me* to build the home health business? I don't know anything about the home health business." His response was simple and straightforward: "But that's what you do around here—you build businesses. So, go learn about it, go build it, or go buy it."

I knew he was right. Even then, disruptive leadership was what I loved to do. I learned it from my parents, on the baseball field, in school, and throughout my professional life. Embarking on difficult research and planning new and challenging strategies was something that had always inspired me. I was cognizant, however, that just because I was becoming more adept at using intentional disruption as a business strategy, it didn't preclude failure. Harvard Business School professor and architect of the "disruptive innovation" theory Clayton Christensen noted that disruption doesn't necessarily ensure success: "A common mistake is to focus on the results achieved—to claim that a company is disruptive by virtue of its success. But success is not built into the definition of disruption: Not every disruptive path leads to a triumph, and not every triumphant newcomer follows a disruptive path."[5] I knew that if I was going to enter the home health sphere, I had to do so deliberately, strategically, and realistically.

Even before our conversation on the plane, I had been thinking hard about the changing landscape of post-acute care. As the Kindred nursing home business continued to struggle, it became apparent that entering the fast-growing arena of home health and hospice might be the provocation Kindred needed. The problem was, we didn't know anything about home health. We needed to build a foundation that would be the catalyst for a significantly disruptive event. I decided that rather than sit back and play defense watching our existing businesses continue to struggle, we should intentionally disrupt the healthcare ecosystem and aggressively enter the home health fray.

---

5   Clayton M. Christensen, Michael E. Raynor, and Rory McDonald, "What Is Disruptive Innovation?" *Harvard Business Review*, December 2015, https://hbr.org/2015/12/what-is-disruptive-innovation.

BE CAREFUL NOT TO WIN THE BATTLE AND LOSE THE WAR

The healthcare dealmaking landscape is littered with the remains of unsuccessful deals. I know of many companies that blindly entered emerging fields without adequate preparation and planning, which ultimately led to large write-offs, bankruptcies, and unemployed CEOs. You simply cannot be disruptive without understanding what you're disrupting. The path is strewn with disrupters who didn't have a real understanding of what the implications of their disruptive actions might be. I was being called to finish the job my predecessors had started—clear the path for a transformation of the company. When we returned from the leadership conference, I got right to it.

> You simply cannot be disruptive without understanding what you're disrupting. The path is strewn with disrupters who didn't have a real understanding of what the implications of their disruptive actions might be.

Starting from scratch, we hired a management team that we built from the ground up. We then laid out a calculated acquisition strategy to build a nucleus of capabilities in the home health space that could serve as the foundation for a larger, more aggressive second phase. First we landed a small $5 million deal and then a larger $10 million deal. Not long after, we acquired a $50 million deal in California. That base of businesses gave us enough confidence to purchase a larger Texas home health company for $75 million, followed by a $100 million deal with a company in Florida. We became adept at integrating new deals, and over the course of two years, we went from not being on anyone's radar to approximately $350 million in revenues. We began building real systems and infrastructure, and we were ready for something even bigger.

In May 2014, Gentiva Health Services, a publicly traded home health and hospice company, had been struggling with its own set of disruptions. The largest provider of home nursing and rehabilitation services in the country was being weighed down by its onerous debt burden and some bad reimbursement news out of Washington, D.C., which had driven its public share price down below seven dollars per share—a historical low point for the company.

After identifying Gentiva as our potential choice, one large problem persisted: the executive leadership and board of directors of their company did not want to sell the business. In most instances going "hostile" on another public company is rife with challenges and rarely works. Hostile takeovers have been equated to old Western movie plots: picture the lonesome cowboy charging through the saloon doors with his gun drawn. The first cowboy usually gets shot. It's the second or third one who canters in and saves the day. If things didn't go exactly as planned, it was likely Kindred would be the first proverbial cowboy in, paving the way for another company to pick up our pieces and save the day.

In healthcare, hostile takeovers are almost unheard of. One of the main challenges in the healthcare arena is that the company being acquired typically isn't just making a widget, for example. Usually—and as was the case with Gentiva—the core foundation of what we were buying was the people: the nurses, the therapists, the culture that makes the product. Even if we won the battle and acquired the company, we could still lose the war when we tried to integrate a business that didn't want to join our organization.

For this reason, my strategy was to foster open communication and relationships with both the employees of Gentiva and the leaders who would ease the post-hostile takeover transition. First, I identified the key leaders who would create stability and continuity in the company going forward. I created back-channel communications with senior team leaders, allowing us to communicate away from the public noise of the deal. When you are attempting something as disruptive as a takeover of a public company, where your widget is people and the product is providing care, you have to maintain stability in the operations and the product itself. If I wasn't able to do that, then being a disrupter would just be disruptive. It wouldn't achieve my end goal, which was to buy the premier home care business in the country—a deal Kindred needed if we were to truly transform our company indefinitely.

I took this same approach with the rank-and-file teammates at Gentiva. Publicly and privately, I established the case that this would be a positive step for their teams. The nonpublic communications I established rallied their company behind the deal, so that if Gentiva's top executive leadership shared biased information, the employee base was already on board with Kindred's mission. In many ways, by the time some of their leaders spoke against the deal with their team, they had already lost their credibility. That is ultimately when they had to give up the fight.

Creating these levels of disruption, however, are not for the faint of heart. In every press release issued, we were thinking about the audience—the employees and the shareholders. Before each one became public, I would use the relationships I had built with key leaders to make sure they knew what was occurring. Nothing was being communicated to the public without their teammates knowing about it first. We established a theme called "Better Together." At the same time I was thinking about our potential new teammates at Gentiva, I also had to think about my current employees and how they might react. It is a complex balancing act that requires a lot of preparation, leadership, and proactive decision-making.

In May 2014, Kindred announced a proposal to acquire Gentiva for $14 a share, representing a 64 percent premium or $1.6 billion in total consideration. The next nine months had more plot twists than a good novel, as seen in the summaries of press releases below. We moved; they countermoved. We pushed; they pulled. Many days I went home feeling certain no deal would be had. All of this played out publicly in the papers and online. Prognosticators and analysts, shareholders, and employees all watched our moves as if they had popcorn at a good movie. I just hoped I could be the first cowboy in *and* the hero. Only time would tell.

TIMELINE OF GENTIVA ACQUISITION

May 15, 2014: "Kindred Healthcare Announces Proposal to Acquire Gentiva Health Services for $14.00 per Share in Cash and Stock, Representing a 64% Premium, in $1.6 Billion Transaction"

LOUISVILLE, KY (May 15, 2014)–Kindred Healthcare, Inc. ("Kindred" or the "Company") (NYSE:KND) today announced a proposal to acquire all of the outstanding shares of common stock of Gentiva Health Services, Inc. ("Gentiva") (NASDAQ:GTIV) for a combination of $7.00 per share in cash and $7.00 of Kindred common stock. Kindred also offered to increase its offer to 100% cash if the Gentiva Board so elects.

May 27, 2014: "Kindred Healthcare Sends Letter to Gentiva Board regarding Gentiva's Adoption of a Poison Pill"

LOUISVILLE, KY (May 27, 2014)–Kindred Healthcare, Inc. ("Kindred" or the "Company") (NYSE:KND) today sent the following letter to the Gentiva Health Services, Inc. ("Gentiva") (NASDAQ:GTIV) Board of Directors in response to the poison pill (also known as a "shareholder rights plan") implemented by the Gentiva Board and disclosed by Gentiva on Friday, May 23, 2014:

Since the May 15, 2014 public announcement of our offer to acquire Gentiva for total consideration of $14.00 per share, we have heard from both companies' shareholders–and sell-side research analysts have reported–that they support a combination and that the price is a very compelling and significant premium to Gentiva's historic trading price and projected earnings estimates...

June 16, 2014: "Kindred Healthcare to Commence All-Cash Tender Offer to Acquire All Outstanding Shares of Gentiva Health Services for $14.50 per Share"

LOUISVILLE, KY (June 16, 2014)—Kindred Healthcare, Inc. ("Kindred" or "the Company") (NYSE:KND) today announced that tomorrow it will commence a cash tender offer to acquire all of the outstanding shares of common stock of Gentiva Health Services, Inc. ("Gentiva") (NASDAQ:GTIV), together with the associated preferred share purchase rights, for $14.50 per share in cash, for a total equity value of approximately $573 million. With the assumption of Gentiva's debt, the transaction would be valued at approximately $1.7 billion.

June 27, 2014: "Kindred Healthcare Sends Letter to Gentiva"

LOUISVILLE, KY (June 27, 2014)—Kindred Healthcare, Inc. ("Kindred" or the "Company") (NYSE:KND) today sent the following letter to the board of directors of Gentiva Health Services, Inc. ("Gentiva") (NASDAQ:GTIV):

We are writing to you, and the entire board of directors of Gentiva, regarding the reports in the marketplace that Gentiva may be pursuing an acquisition of Amedisys (NASDAQ:AMED). We are concerned that, while refusing to discuss Kindred's highly attractive cash offer, the Gentiva board may be pursuing a course that would disenfranchise its shareholders through a value-destroying and highly levered transaction with Amedisys...

June 30, 2014: "Gentiva Board Unanimously Rejects Unsolicited Tender Offer from Kindred"

ATLANTA (BUSINESS WIRE)—Gentiva Health Services, Inc. (the "Company or "Gentiva") (NASDAQ:GTIV) announced today that its Board of Directors (the "Board"), after careful consideration and consultation with its financial and legal advisors, unanimously determined to reject the unsolicited, highly conditional tender offer from Kindred Healthcare, Inc. ("Kindred") (NYSE:KND) to acquire all of the outstanding shares of Gentiva, together with the associated preferred share purchase rights, for a price of $14.50 per share in cash (the "Offer"). The Board determined that the Offer is not in the best interests of Gentiva or its stockholders as it significantly undervalues the Company and, as such, the Board recommends that Gentiva stockholders reject the Offer and not tender their shares into the Offer. The Board noted that the consideration offered to stockholders pursuant to the Offer is not significantly different from Kindred's previous unsolicited proposals made on April 14 and May 5, 2014, both of which Gentiva's Board unanimously rejected after careful consideration.

July 1, 2014: "Kindred Healthcare Responds to Gentiva"

LOUISVILLE, KY (July 1, 2014)—Kindred Healthcare, Inc. ("Kindred" or the "Company") (NYSE:KND) today responded to the decision by the board of directors of Gentiva Health Services, Inc. ("Gentiva") (NASDAQ:GTIV) recommending against Kindred's offer to acquire all of Gentiva's outstanding common stock for $14.50 per share in cash.

July 14, 2014: "Kindred Healthcare Increases All-Cash Tender Offer for Gentiva to $16.00 per Share"

LOUISVILLE, KY (July 14, 2014)—Kindred Healthcare, Inc. ("Kindred" or the "Company") (NYSE:KND) today announced that it has amended its previously announced all-cash tender offer to acquire all of the outstanding shares of common stock of Gentiva Health Services, Inc. ("Gentiva") (NASDAQ:GTIV), together with the associated preferred share purchase rights.

July 14, 2014: "Gentiva Urges Shareholders to Take No Action in Response to Tender Offer Amendment Announcement by Kindred"

ATLANTA (BUSINESS WIRE)–Gentiva Health Services, Inc. (NASDAQ:GTIV) today noted that Kindred Healthcare, Inc. (NYSE:KND) has announced a revised tender offer to acquire 14.9% of the outstanding shares of Gentiva common stock for $16.00 per share in cash. The closing price of Gentiva common stock on Friday, July 11 was $15.82 per share.

July 17, 2014: "Gentiva Board of Directors Unanimously Rejects Kindred's Amended Partial Tender Offer; Announces Receipt of Alternative Proposal"

ATLANTA (BUSINESS WIRE)–Gentiva Health Services, Inc. (NASDAQ:GTIV) announced today that its Board of Directors (the "Board"), after careful consideration and consultation with its financial and legal advisors, unanimously determined to reject the partial tender offer from Kindred Healthcare, Inc. ("Kindred") (NYSE:KND) to acquire 14.9% of the outstanding shares of Gentiva for a price of $16.00 per share in cash (the "Offer"). The Board determined that the Offer significantly undervalues Gentiva's shares, is coercive and not in the best interests of Gentiva stockholders. Accordingly, the Board recommends that Gentiva stockholders reject the Offer and not tender their shares into the Offer.

July 21, 2014: "Kindred Healthcare Sends Letter to the Gentiva Board of Directors"

LOUISVILLE, KY (July 21, 2014)–Kindred Healthcare, Inc. ("Kindred" or the "Company") (NYSE:KND) today sent the following letter to the board of directors of Gentiva Health Services, Inc. ("Gentiva") (NASDAQ:GTIV) in response to Gentiva's announcement on July 17, 2014 that an unnamed party has purportedly submitted a proposal to acquire Gentiva for $17.25 per share, subject to financing, due diligence, internal approvals and other conditions.

I am writing following the recent discussions among our respective financial advisors in response to the press release issued by Gentiva on July 17, 2014, which stated that an unnamed party has submitted a proposal to acquire the company for $17.25 per share in cash, subject to financing, due diligence, internal approvals and other conditions...

July 21, 2014: "Gentiva Health Services Announces Receipt of Acquisition Proposal from Kindred Healthcare"

ATLANTA (BUSINESS WIRE)–Gentiva Health Services, Inc. (NASDAQ:GTIV) ("Gentiva") today announced that it has received a conditional proposal from Kindred Healthcare, Inc. ("Kindred") (NYSE:KND) to acquire all of the outstanding shares of Gentiva common stock for $17.25 per share. Kindred has indicated that this proposal is subject to "diligence to confirm that such additional value is warranted." Gentiva's Board of Directors, in consultation with its financial and legal advisors, will review the proposal carefully in due course.

July 24, 2014: "Gentiva Health Services Announces Entry into Nondisclosure Agreement"

ATLANTA (BUSINESS WIRE)–Gentiva Health Services, Inc. (NASDAQ:GTIV) ("Gentiva" or the "Company") today announced that it has entered into a nondisclosure agreement with the recognized owner, operator and investor who, as disclosed previously, delivered on July 17, 2014 a proposal to Gentiva's board of directors (the "Board") to acquire all outstanding shares of Gentiva common stock for $17.25 per share in cash, subject to certain conditions.

July 28, 2014: "Kindred Healthcare Announces Expiration of Tender Offer for Gentiva"

LOUISVILLE, KY (July 28, 2014)–Kindred Healthcare, Inc. ("Kindred" or "the Company") (NYSE:KND) today announced the expiration of its amended tender offer to purchase 14.9% of the outstanding shares of Gentiva Health Services, Inc. ("Gentiva") (NASDAQ:GTIV) for $16.00 per share in cash. At the expiration of the offer, certain conditions of the offer had not been satisfied and Kindred had not waived those conditions. Accordingly, no shares of common stock of Gentiva were purchased by Kindred pursuant to the offer, and all tendered shares will be returned promptly. Kindred is prepared to enter into appropriate confidentiality and standstill agreements with Gentiva in order to facilitate discussions regarding the proposed combination of Kindred and Gentiva.

July 29, 2014: "Kindred Healthcare Reiterates Commitment to All-Cash Acquisition of Gentiva for $17.25 Per Share"

LOUISVILLE, KY (July 29, 2014)–Kindred Healthcare, Inc. ("Kindred") (NYSE:KND) today reiterated its commitment to its proposed combination with Gentiva Health Services, Inc. ("Gentiva") (NASDAQ:GTIV).

October 9, 2014: "Kindred and Gentiva Reach Definitive Agreement Creating Nation-Wide Integrated Care Delivery System Preferred by Consumers and Payors"

LOUISVILLE, KY, and ATLANTA (October 9, 2014)–Kindred Healthcare, Inc. ("Kindred" or the "Company") (NYSE:KND) and Gentiva Health Services, Inc. ("Gentiva") (NASDAQ:GTIV) today announced that the companies have entered into a definitive merger agreement under which Kindred will acquire all of the outstanding shares of Gentiva common stock for $19.50 per share in a combination of cash and stock. The agreement was unanimously approved by the boards of directors of both companies.

Under the terms of the agreement, Gentiva shareholders will receive $14.50 per share in cash and $5.00 of Kindred common stock (which equates to 1.257 shares of Kindred common stock based upon an agreed upon fixed exchange ratio). The transaction is valued at $1.8 billion, including the assumption of net debt. The companies expect the closing of the transaction to occur in the first quarter of 2015.

The combination of Kindred and Gentiva will further enhance Kindred's industry leading position as the Nation's premier post-acute and rehabilitation services provider and make Kindred at Home the largest and most geographically diversified Home Health and Hospice organization in the United States.

December 18, 2014: "Kindred Healthcare Closes $1.35 Billion Senior Unsecured Notes Offering; Announces February 2 Target Closing Date for Merger with Gentiva Now That All Financing Is Complete"

LOUISVILLE, KY (December 18, 2014)–Kindred Healthcare, Inc. ("Kindred" or the "Company") (NYSE:KND) today announced that it has closed its previously announced offering of $1.35 billion aggregate principal amount of senior unsecured notes. The $1.35 billion of notes were issued in two tranches of $750 million of 8.00% Senior Notes due 2020 at an issue price of 100% and $600 million of 8.75% Senior Notes due 2023 at an issue price of 100% (collectively, the "Notes").

With the completion of this notes offering, Kindred has all necessary financing in place to fund its previously announced acquisition of Gentiva Health Services, Inc. ("Gentiva") (NASDAQ:GTIV). Kindred and Gentiva are now targeting a February 2, 2015 closing date, subject to satisfaction of the conditions to closing under the merger agreement between Kindred and Gentiva.

January 22, 2015: "Gentiva Health Services Stockholders Approve Combination with Kindred Healthcare"

ATLANTA (BUSINESS WIRE)–Gentiva Health Services, Inc. (NASDAQ:GTIV) ("Gentiva" or the "Company") today announced that all proposals necessary for the combination with Kindred Healthcare, Inc. (NYSE:KND) ("Kindred") were approved by Gentiva's stockholders at the Company's Special Meeting of Stockholders held today. Gentiva and Kindred expect to complete the transaction on February 2, 2015.

January 22, 2015: "Kindred Healthcare Announces Gentiva Health Services Stockholder Approval of Combination"

LOUISVILLE, KY (January 22, 2015)–Kindred Healthcare, Inc. ("Kindred" or the "Company") (NYSE:KND) announced that, at the Special Meeting of Stockholders of Gentiva Health Services, Inc. ("Gentiva") (NASDAQ:GTIV) held today, the Gentiva stockholders approved Gentiva's combination with Kindred.

February 2, 2015: "Kindred Healthcare Completes Acquisition of Gentiva Health Services Creating Nation-Wide Integrated Care Delivery System"

LOUISVILLE, KY (February 2, 2015)–Kindred Healthcare, Inc. ("Kindred" or the "Company") (NYSE:KND) today announced that it has completed its acquisition of Gentiva Health Services, Inc. ("Gentiva"), in a transaction valued at $1.8 billion, including the assumption of net debt.

* * *

Finally, in February 2015, Kindred wore Gentiva down and formally announced our acquisition of the company and our closing of the deal. The total consideration we agreed to was $1.8 billion, which was a record amount for a home health company at the time. (This acquisition that disrupted the status quo and countered the changing macro environment in healthcare allowed me to make the aggressive decision, two years later, to exit our skilled nursing business, which we will discuss fully in chapter 5.) That $1.8 billion buyout created a significant premium return for our shareholders when we sold the same business to Humana and a group of private equity partners just three and a half years later.

Had we not aggressively pursued the disruptive and nearly impossible feat of pulling off a hostile public takeover of Gentiva, Kindred would have had a vastly different future: first, Kindred would not have had the financial wherewithal to exit the skilled nursing business two years later; second, Kindred would not have been viewed as interesting enough to take private; and third, without the first two, Kindred would have likely faced a difficult financial reckoning in its near future.

If Kindred had remained in a defensive stance, there would be no growth or expansion, and the healthcare landscape would continue to be rife with the passive, untenable deals of the past. When planned and executed to perfection, intentional disruption—even against long odds—can be the offensive jolt a company needs to execute a successful transformation that positions it for sustained success.

LESSONS FOR THE
INTENTIONAL DISRUPTER

- If you're going to disrupt, have stable counterbalances at the ready—in the forms of stable leadership and a supportive workforce.

- If you decide to intentionally disrupt, as in a public hostile takeover, you had better be prepared to go all the way. If you're not, don't start.

- It's not a short-term goal; it's a long-term strategy. Plan for day two.

CHAPTER 5

WHEN IT'S TIME TO SAY GOODBYE

IT WAS EARLY AUGUST 2011, and my family and I were starting our annual summer vacation. With my wife in the passenger seat and my young children in the backseat, we were excitedly driving toward our home in Southern California.

Suddenly, I received a priority notification on my phone. I quickly handed it to my wife beside me to read aloud: "CMS has issued a decision to roll back reimbursement in our nursing home business by 11.5 percent." My chest tightened, and my heart pounded. I had hoped this day would never come. I had to pull off to the side of Interstate 405 and gather myself. This was bad. Very bad.

We had known for some time that the government was preparing to inflict a blow on the SNF industry, so we had worked tirelessly with the American Health Care Association (AHCA) to establish what we believed the appropriate, proactive approach might be. We had offered a suggestion of how the industry could handle reimbursement in a more business-friendly manner that would protect residents and employee salaries while still getting the government what it wanted. With this end in mind, we had proposed that a rate cut be blended in over the course of four years. This seemed doable for us, but getting the nursing center industry—which could be described at times as tribal with all its differing states and regions—to agree had proven difficult. Because of this, it was hard to gain consensus on a deal with the AHCA. In a disappointing and painful move, without industry cohesion on a better solution, the government unilaterally decided to impose an 11.5 percent rate cut all at once.

For Kindred, with $1.5 billion of skilled nursing Medicare exposure, this move amounted to a more than $150 million hit to our bottom line. A rate cut of this magnitude represented nearly two-thirds of the entire profitability of the Kindred enterprise. The company would face massive financial repercussions if immediate changes were not made.

Leaders running companies in volatile business sectors like healthcare often face unexpected external disruptions that can impair operations and immobilize decision-making. The temptation is to blame results on these external forces. Even if true, this approach is not a formula for long-term success, and it's not part of my DNA. Reaching into my past, I remembered my mother reminding us when things didn't go our way that "Breiers don't wallow." So I didn't.

I determined at that very moment to go on offense and become intentionally disruptive. First, through a difficult but necessary restructuring of our company, I found a path to cut tens of millions of dollars of company costs in one year without compromising the quality of care delivered to our patients or Kindred's mission. This in and of itself was massively disruptive, but I didn't feel it would be enough. I knew the answer was a full and final exit from the challenging nursing center business. What I didn't know was how I would get there or when.

A disruptive action, taken unilaterally against one's interests and without really having an opportunity to control its outcome, can put a company, a CEO, or just about anyone on their back. It's easy to get swallowed up in the difficulties a disruption of this nature can create. As I would soon learn, it can at times be discombobulating, disheartening, unnerving, and downright painful.

NEGOTIATING WITH YOUR LANDLORD

Anyone who has ever dealt with a landlord knows it is not always an easy dynamic. What happens, for example, if after one year you no longer want to live in an apartment you rented for a five-year term? Or worse, you can't afford the rent, but you still have a five-year term. You understand that just because you might want to make a change, that doesn't necessarily mean your landlord agrees to let you out of your lease. This was essentially my predicament in working with Kindred's largest SNF landlord, Ventas.

Ventas had grown increasingly powerful over the two decades since Vencor's bankruptcy and subsequent reorganization into Kindred. Though Kindred was the operating company, Ventas held a great deal of power as the REIT (real estate investment trust), which in effect made them the landlord. Ventas had a series of airtight master lease provisions that made negotiating any changes to the agreement's terms nearly impossible. Hidden in the lease terms, for example, was something even more prohibitive than the leases themselves: due to a combative postbankruptcy negotiation in 1999, Ventas had a right of consent provision written into the SNF leases that granted them unilateral right to overrule any strategic "change of control" Kindred might want to engage in. This provision ensured that Kindred's board never really controlled its own rights or future. In other words, if Kindred wanted to sell itself, sell its business, or change the makeup of its structure, Ventas had the right to simply say no! Sounds just like a tough landlord, right? I knew it was time to say goodbye to the nursing center business, but it wasn't going to be as easy as just deciding I wanted to do it.

As the third quarter of 2016 came to a close, the SNF business at Kindred was operating at larger and larger financial losses. This was due in large part to the continued dramatic reduction in reimbursement the industry had been burdened with over many previous years. Kindred was simply not willing to cut costs to the point where quality of patient care would suffer. It appeared the third-quarter public guidance goals were going to fall short and annual guidance for the remainder of the year would need a significant downward revision.

There were massive issues within the skilled nursing industry that seemed to be falling apart right in front of our eyes. Companies were declaring bankruptcy all around us. There was litigation amid a terrible regulatory environment. I remember thinking to myself, "If I just sit here and do nothing, we are going to get our butts kicked and possibly go out of business." Playing defense or making incremental changes on the margin wouldn't cut it. Facing massive amounts of disruption to Kindred's stock price, I knew I had to take dramatic steps to permanently get out of the SNF business.

The first and most important step a public company CEO must take when they want to be intentionally disruptive is to make sure that there is total alignment with the board of directors. I've had numerous previous CEOs tell me that at the end of the day, the only thing that really matters is that your board stands behind you. To this end, I met with bankers, lawyers, and consultants and built a team of advisors to help me formulate a plan. After preparing for months, I headed to Austin, Texas, for what would be a defining meeting with my board. It felt like I was readying for battle for the company's survival. And I was.

Once I am in an aggressive, offensive posture, I always find myself to be calm, assertive, and confident—much the same way I felt when I stepped into the batter's box after hours of preparation. I felt good. I had a strong plan. We were taking the fight to the enemy—the enemy being inertia and external disruptions. I knew if I tried and wasn't successful convincing the board of my intentions, I'd try again until we found common ground on which to agree. I fear failure, and I hate to lose, but I'm not debilitated by it.

At that critical meeting, I gave our board a clear and decisive view of what the company was facing. I told them that whatever the cost, whatever the price that needed to be paid, we had to find a way to definitively divest ourselves of this business. Any good leader knows that pointing out a problem is not helpful unless it comes with a suggested solution, so I assured them I had a plan to turn a negative into a positive.

It wasn't obvious to all the board members that exiting the SNF business in its entirety was altogether necessary. Some were skeptical about whether we could get Ventas to acquiesce. I explained that failure to do so at this critical juncture could put the entire financial enterprise of our company in jeopardy. I laid out a specific plan to engage Ventas, to negotiate a deal, and to manage the public relations and communications issues we would face on Wall Street. I knew executing this plan would be one of the most difficult challenges I or any CEO would have to face. At the end of a long meeting, I had the unanimous support of my board to move forward. I walked out with my marching orders and thought, "Now it's time to do this."

A FULL AND FINAL EXIT

With my board of directors now firmly behind me, I began to engage Ventas in a protracted negotiation. They weren't required to do anything, let alone let us out of our leases, so I had to come up with a creative solution to buy our way out of the skilled nursing business. As a landlord, Ventas used their contractual leverage to repeatedly refuse to engage in a meaningful negotiation. At one point, I told my team I didn't care what the bid ask was; I was simply determined to get Ventas to propose a number—any number. I had believed for some time that getting a number on the table for the first time, even if massively unattainable, would at least give me a chance to negotiate a solution. At the time, we had internally valued the entirety of the SNF portfolio around $700–$800 million. If we could agree on anything close to that, I could find a way to finish the deal.

After multiple intensive sessions of round-the-clock meetings, Kindred and Ventas finally came to an agreement: Kindred would pay Ventas $700 million for the right to exit the SNF business. The high price came with one final caveat on Kindred's behalf: Kindred had the right to exercise our change of control without Ventas's consent should we ever decide to sell the company or take it private. This was the concession I needed to put Kindred on a path toward controlling our own destiny, and this was the key to my being able to devise an intentionally disruptive plan to secure Kindred's viability into the future.

They agreed. We had done it; we had finally negotiated our full exit from the SNF business that had been weighing us down for so long. Most importantly, we had used the negotiation to buy our company's freedom, now and forever. The most significant negotiation in Kindred's long history had come to an end. We had turned an externally disruptive event into an opportunity to define our own future. Now, we needed to tell Wall Street all about it.

THE LONG GAME

I've always looked at challenges on and off the field like a nine-inning game. Unlike almost any other sport, baseball has no clock. There is no time limit on completing the game. Until you've finished, the game must be played in its entirety. Whether you are winning big or losing badly, you have to play the second, third, fourth inning, all the way to the end. Both on the field and in the boardroom, there are many moves that have to be made and you have to keep going until you're finished. Getting the board behind me was just one inning of what would turn out to be a game that went far into extra innings.

Even in the best of times, dealing with Wall Street can be complicated, with activist shareholders, unfriendly sell-side analysts, and short-term holders of company stock who demand immediate returns. Managing "the Street" proactively after a bad quarter is one of the toughest jobs a public company CEO has to do. Being Kindred's CEO is no different.

With my board of directors behind me and the deal with Ventas firmly in sight, I decided to utilize the scale of intentional disruption to go on offense and try to turn a negative situation into one that might be viewed as a positive. Using the disruptive strategies already outlined in previous chapters, my team and I—supported by a group of our advisors who specialized in these situations—devised a plan. We decided to proactively and intentionally disrupt the status quo that most watchers of our stock had grown accustomed to. The path was now clear to go from defense to offense.

Through a series of clear and determined communication tools, including our third-quarter earnings release and subsequent public call, I didn't focus on the difficulties of the quarter itself and the fact that we had agreed to pay Ventas $700 million without knowing for certain whether we would generate enough proceeds to get our money back. When I put our earnings release out on November 7, 2016, I had not even formally completed my negotiation with Ventas yet. Even though I did not have a signed deal, I was confident I would get it done, so I decided to tell the story the way I wanted the story told.

Remembering the transparent communication strategies I used successfully during our Gentiva acquisition, I wanted to speak to our team to assure them of their stability even in a disruptive atmosphere. During our earnings call, I reminded participants that we would continue to put our people first:

> *I think what was very clear for us was that, notwithstanding a lot of work we're doing behind the scenes, the most important thing for us was when we made this announcement yesterday, we wanted our employees, our teammates, our partners to be the first ones to hear it, not anybody else. So in terms of process and things that have become public, it was very important to me, and to our board, and to the rest of our management team that we treat our employees the right way by making sure that they knew what was happening before anybody else did.*[6]

From the time the board meeting ended to the time the earnings release circulated, I tried to get Ventas to agree to a deal, but I couldn't. Again using the strategies that had served me well during the Gentiva acquisition, I made sure to maintain direct communication with

---

6   Ben Breier, president and CEO, Kindred Healthcare Inc., transcript from KND Q3 2016 Kindred Healthcare Inc. earnings call, November 8, 2016.

key leaders, in this case the CEO of Ventas. I said, "Ventas has clear consent rights to any action we make. We can't do anything without them, and our intention is not to do anything without them."[7] I knew Ventas leaders would see this, and I didn't want them to feel backed into a corner. I had to use the call to continue to enrich and develop this strategic alliance.

At the same time that I was navigating how our team members and Ventas leaders would react, I also tried to appeal to the shareholders in the company. I had to remind them that we were continuing to make Kindred Healthcare a more viable and valuable investment:

> *I know investors have a lot of questions...and I assure you, we are giving a lot of thought and a lot of time and effort to how we will balance the selling of nursing centers, the reduction of overhead, the management of cash—all the various things we are working on doing. But a reminder for investors, that at the end of the day, notwithstanding some of the bumps to get from here to there, when investors wake up to a Kindred Healthcare that no longer has exposure to the skilled nursing facility business, that has $70 million to $100 million of overhead taken out of its SG&A infrastructure, has better free cash flow, and better earning characteristics, this is going to be a company that shareholders are going to be more happy to own a share of in the future than they even are today. So we'll get through the process, and we'll work with our partners on this, and we've got a lot of work to do. [8]*

On November 14, 2016, we put out a press release announcing to the world that we had finally formalized our plan:

---

7   Ibid.

8   Kindred Healthcare, "Kindred Agrees with Ventas Facilitating Strategic Exit," 2016.

We are pleased with these mutually beneficial agreements with Ventas that allow us to fully exit the skilled nursing facility business in an expedited manner. We expect our exit from the skilled nursing facility business to be accretive to earnings and to substantially improve our cash flow generation and leverage profile going forward. As announced previously, we expect our associated cost realignment initiative to eliminate approximately $70 million to $100 million of costs, which includes approximately $60 million of direct costs associated with our nursing center division with the balance primarily derived from reductions of indirect costs in our shared service support centers. The agreements with Ventas represent an important step forward in the success of this initiative.[9]

We had now negotiated a deal, we had announced a deal, and we were committed to doing a deal that we made public. Unfortunately, there was one major problem remaining: even though we had an agreement with Ventas on the price to exit the SNF business, I didn't know if I would be able to find the $700 million to pay them. Furthermore, I wouldn't really know whether I had the money until I actually went to sell the business. There were a lot of people on my team who reminded me that I could get fired for this and that there were hundreds of ways this could go wrong. They were certainly right, but I did it anyway. There was no plan B; this was "plan all."

After an agonizingly difficult process, our stock actually traded up after the news broke. More importantly, ten days after announcing our deal to exit the SNFs in their entirety, Kindred received an unsolicited offer from a large private equity firm proposing to take the company private at a significant premium to where the stock price was trading.

---

9   Ibid.

This was amazing news for our company, and it was validating for me as a leader and disrupter. All the time and preparation that went into this complicated, long game paid off enormously. Now, with the prospect of better days ahead, I had to turn all my focus on getting the SNFs sold and generating the $700 million of proceeds I knew I needed to pay Ventas to exit this business permanently.

DIVESTING THE BUSINESS

The amount of work it took to finally go to market and begin the process of selling the skilled nursing business had been colossal. During this time, I often recalled Winston Churchill's moving speech at London's Mansion House during World War II: "This is not the end. This is not even the beginning of the end. But it is perhaps the end of the beginning."[10] These words followed me as I began the difficult task of divesting an entire business.

Much as we had done previously on large transactions, we started the process of selling the nursing home business by creating a Project Management Office (PMO). This PMO would be responsible for sourcing prospective buyers, funneling thousands of pages of data, and providing the diligence needed to value the assets. We also needed a team of lawyers and bankers that would help us navigate the deal. Having announced our intention to sell the business publicly in November 2016, it was our stated goal to find a buyer by the middle of 2017.

Having already agreed to pay Ventas $700 million for their share of the business, we knew we had to find a buyer willing to at least match that. The current balance sheet at Kindred, the amount of cash

---

10 "Churchill: 'This Is Not the End' (Nov. 1942)," video, 0:13, Tototo981, May 15, 2010, https://www.youtube.com/watch?v=pdRH5wzCQQw.

available, and the prospect of borrowing more money to pay off the deal all seemed prohibitive. We needed to find a way to generate the proceeds necessary to pay the $700 million. What we didn't know was whether there were any buyers willing to pay the price. The intentionally disruptive action I had taken to exit the SNF business had approached its zero hour.

We began the process by casting a wide net in search of prospective buyers. Early on, we were excited about a potential partner who appeared willing to pay $150 million more than anyone else had offered. The thought of generating this kind of return was thrilling. The additional cash proceeds this bid could generate could be a game changer for our company moving forward. Not surprisingly, this exciting prospect did not come from the U.S. ranks. It was a Chinese firm that, like many of their Asian counterparts, had been seeking ways to take money out of mainland China and put it to work in the safer harbors of America.

As the deal gained momentum, President Donald Trump announced a new aggressive approach on trade and other transactions with China. Trump and his advisors came down on Chinese investment in America with the weight of the entire U.S. government. For companies like our bidder, what had already been an incredibly tricky task of getting money out of China to the United States became nearly impossible. Kindred was one of many American companies at the time working on a Chinese deal—only to see it die upon the sword of an international trade debate.

With the Chinese out of the process, we were left with two domestic bidders, both of which had advantages and disadvantages. I was looking for the deal that would give us not only the maximum return, but, equally important, the most realistic chance to get across the finish line and close our transaction.

After an incredibly tense and difficult few months, we finally struck a deal with a large private equity firm that had been in and out of the skilled nursing business for years. This agreement would bring Kindred's total value of the sale to approximately $915 million. This sum would allow us to pay $700 million to Ventas, keep some proceeds for ourselves to use in other parts of our business, and most importantly, exit the business we had promised investors we were going to exit to meet our commitments. It had been an enormous gamble, years in the making, but we had done it. Our intentionally disruptive actions had freed the way for better days to come at Kindred.

* * *

In retrospect, my decision to turn an external disruption within our business into an opportunity to transform the company by exiting the SNF space and unshackling us from the onerous and restrictive lease provisions cleared the path for the much more intentionally disruptive decision to take the company private. Being forced to take decisive action because of an externally disruptive event enabled me to tap into my natural inclination to be intentionally disruptive.

Our subsequent deal to ultimately sell the company and take it private—with a different buyer from the original bidder—was a direct result of intentional disruption and allowed me to accomplish a complex transaction. This early-inning disruption ultimately set us up for the

> Being forced to take decisive action because of an externally disruptive event enabled me to tap into my natural inclination to be intentionally disruptive.

endgame. If ever I needed reassurance that my intentional disruption techniques were powerful strategy tools, I had it. I have continued to use these skills to create, manage, and dispel disruptions for Kindred Healthcare.

I realize that the disruption techniques I used to exit the skilled nursing business were risky and could have led to my professional demise, but sometimes you have to do it anyway. When your back is against the wall and you're in a corner, there is only one way out. You can't wait for someone to come help you; you can't wait for good luck; you can't wait for divine intervention. You must gather your strength and faculties and come out of that corner swinging. You have to punch your way out of that corner. You have to fight like your career depends on it, because in a disruptive market like ours, it just might.

LESSONS ON PREPARING FOR IMPENDING DISRUPTIONS

- Disruption is a team sport. You can want to change the world, but you can't do it by yourself.

- Don't introduce the problem without offering a solution.

- Prepare for the long game; large disruptions tend to play out over longer periods of time.

- If you're backed into a corner, be prepared to punch your way out.

CHAPTER 6

JUST WHEN YOU THINK ALL IS WELL

THE J.P. MORGAN HEALTH CARE CONFERENCE is a massive annual event held in the humid hills of San Francisco. Each January, more than sixty thousand bankers, lawyers, headhunters, private equity partners, hedge fund managers, investors, and executives make the pilgrimage to Northern California to engage in what feels like healthcare's version of Woodstock.

In January 2017, two months after our exit from the skilled nursing facility business, I was one of the many healthcare executives making the rounds among the ensemble cast—shaking hands, kissing babies, selling the Kindred story to anyone who would listen. The weather in the Bay Area is always a bit unpredictable, but this particular year was the wettest and worst anyone could remember in more than thirty years. For three days, it rained sideways, making San Francisco nearly impossible to navigate. Despite nature's action outside, the real action took place inside the conference—every side corridor, coffee shop, outdoor patio, and surrounding hotel was overtaken by people talking about the business of healthcare.

As is typical for a public company CEO, I was overscheduled, overbooked, and overextended trying to meet with everyone I needed to see. Ever since we put out a public release on November 7, 2016, announcing our exit from the skilled nursing facility business, I had hoped things would calm down. And they did—for about a week— then the storm rolled in.

Ten days after telling the public about our plan, our board had received an unsolicited proposal from one of the largest private equity firms in the world to buy Kindred outright and take the company private. I had immediately notified our board of directors, and they in turn had called for an all-hands meeting. During this discussion, the board decided to establish a transaction committee. This four-member team was designated by the broader board to evaluate the seriousness of the proposal, the possibility of other interested parties, and the best price we could garner for the company, should we decide to sell. It didn't mean we were deciding to do anything, but it was critical that we were proactively establishing a process.

While the transaction committee began its work, including engaging with bankers and beginning to talk with other interested parties, I was still managing the disruption we had created less than two weeks prior with the nursing center exit announcement. Now, two months after my disruptive decision to exit the skilled nursing facility business, I was surrounded by the frenetic hustle of the J.P. Morgan conference staring down a long, full day of meetings.

One meeting that had drawn particular interest was with a group of executives from Humana, one of the largest insurance companies in the world. Kindred and Humana had always had a bit of a contentious relationship. As more of the Medicare population was choosing to join the private Medicare Advantage ranks, Humana had grown all-powerful over the providers who delivered the care directly to their members. More often than not, providers like Kindred were engaged in what could sometimes be difficult and painful negotiations. Humana almost always held the upper hand as they utilized the adage "He who owns the gold discharges where it will be spent."

I was happy to find out that the meeting between Humana and Kindred had been scheduled in my hotel suite, meaning I wouldn't have to go out and fight the heavy downpours. As I sat down to discuss what I assumed would be a broad discussion on how Kindred and Humana could collaborate on various business initiatives, I reminded myself how odd it was that the Humana executive team had been willing to come to me. As big and complex as Kindred was, Humana had always cast a large shadow on the healthcare marketplace due to its dominant position in the fast-growing Medicare Advantage world they operated in. With a nearly $50 billion market capitalization and a ranking near the top of the Fortune 500 list, Humana executives did not usually go out of their way to pay a social visit—especially on someone else's turf.

Once the teams had assembled in my suite, general pleasantries were exchanged, including both parties noting the irony of meeting in San Francisco when our respective corporate headquarters were literally down the street in Louisville, Kentucky. Over the course of an hour and a half, Kindred's four business lines were examined with precision. As the curious meeting ended and the Humana executives left the room, my colleague leaned over and exclaimed, "I think they want to buy the company!"

Shortly after the J.P. Morgan conference, a representative from Humana requested that I call the CEO of Humana to discuss potential collaborations involving Kindred and Humana. During that call, I indicated that Kindred was in the process of exploring strategic alternatives, and I explained that I wasn't entirely sure if I had gauged our earlier conversation correctly, but if I had and if Humana wanted to be involved, he should let me know over the next couple of days. He immediately responded, "I don't need a couple of days. We want to be involved." I informed my board chairwoman of Humana's interest, and she agreed that we should obtain the transaction committee's approval to include Humana in the process.

My plan to intentionally disrupt the status quo for the benefit of all our stakeholders had now been put into hyperdrive. To use a popular Kentucky phrase, "We were off to the races"—or so I thought. No business leader could have imagined that the meeting with Humana would begin an epic eighteen-month struggle in which I would have to overcome an act of God, an act of government, and an act of greed.

ACT OF GOD

In 1992, I was a carefree college junior navigating the streets of Philadelphia as a student at the University of Pennsylvania. In August, I decided to return to my home in Miami, Florida, to soak in summer's remaining sun and boating opportunities before starting my senior year of college.

Growing up in South Florida creates an acute awareness of the summer hurricane season, so I knew returning to the coast in August was risky. When I was young, we never had snow days off from school, but "hurricane days" happened frequently. It had been nearly thirty years since South Florida had been hit by a major category five storm. In the summer of 1992, however, as I settled back into my childhood home, Hurricane Andrew loomed in the eastern Caribbean.

In what turned out to be the most expensive natural disaster to ever hit the United States to date, Hurricane Andrew came bulldozing threw southern Miami. The night of the storm was one of the most harrowing of my life. My parents and I wound up spending more than six hours in total darkness huddled together in a small walk-in closet as the roof over our heads blew off, rain and wind poured down on us, and we wondered aloud if we would make it to see the light of morning. Thankfully we did, but this memory flashed before me each and every summer as hurricane season came and went with varying degrees of damage.

Twenty-five years later, as August 2017 approached, I was dealing with a different type of storm. I was engaged in complex negotiations to try to save Kindred from the weight of its enormous debt burden by selling it to a variety of potential buyers, including the consortium of Humana; Texas Pacific Group (TPG); and Welsh, Carson, Anderson & Stowe (WCAS). The deal flow had been choppy to say the least and had in fact died multiple deaths before being revived each time to live another day.

Against this backdrop, Kindred had entered into a sensitive period of intense negotiations. We recognized that keeping the business performance of our core operations on track was critical to getting the deal over the finish line. It was understood that any variations in performance could spook the potential buyers from continuing forward with the transaction. I knew this was a crucial time and recalled economic historian Joseph Schumpeter's warning: "Situations emerge in the process of creative destruction in which many firms may have to perish that nevertheless would be able to live on vigorously and usefully if they could weather a particular storm."[11] I knew I would need to maintain stability and clarity during the impending tempests, for my team and my company.

---

11   Joseph A. Schumpeter, *Capitalism, Socialism and Democracy* (New York: Harper Perennial, 2008), 90.

As the 2017 hurricane season once again approached, I felt that familiar anxiousness return. At the time, two of Kindred's largest states of operation were Texas and Florida. With more than $1.6 billion of annual revenue between the two states, any disruption to the sites would be problematic. Additionally, Kindred employed more than twenty-five thousand teammates between the two states, with thousands of patients entrusted to our care. For this reason, Kindred had always prepared for natural disaster disruptions by being proactive in our emergency response strategies. In August, Hurricane Harvey strengthened and approached the Texas Gulf, and I felt confident that our teams were ready.

Ever since Hurricane Katrina hit New Orleans in 2005, the hospital and post-acute industry has dealt with post-traumatic stress disorder around hurricane planning. The citywide effects were devastating and far-reaching, particularly for the healthcare providers who were unprepared. It was an unmitigated disaster for many hospitals and nursing homes. Evacuations weren't done effectively, and many people died as a result. Some company executives were even criminally charged for negligence. It was a lesson in what not to do in a storm, not just in preparation but also in real-time decision-making that could be the difference between life and death for individuals. If things on the ground were handled wrong, it could also be the demise of a company. These issues remained at the forefront of our minds as Hurricane Harvey made landfall.

What no one could foresee, of course, was the debilitating power and destruction Harvey would unleash on the state. Five straight days of torrential rain and flooding brought the city of Houston—and the ten hospitals we operated there—to its knees. We had multiple problems we had to deal with. The value of human life is paramount to anything else, of course, but as CEO, I had to also consider the broader strategic interests of the company. First and foremost, my primary concern was the safety and well-being of our patients, our employees, and their families. Second, we worried if our hospitals would have enough power, medical supplies, food and water, and staff to continue operations. Last, though unimportant compared to human life, was our concern that a prolonged shutdown of our operations brought on by Mother Nature's disruption could create enough financial damage that the deal we had been working on so hard might be ruined.

Right in the middle of Hurricane Harvey's destruction, we had a scheduled senior management meeting. Our senior leadership team knew that a big transaction was in progress, and this was my opportunity to brief them. Given what was happening in Texas, however, there was a real debate about whether or not we should hold this meeting. We knew the Texas team could not attend the meeting because they were dealing with a major crisis. In addition, many other senior executives were involved in helping to manage the catastrophe, so they were already overextended. The executive committee of the company—the ten most senior members of Kindred's management team—were split on how they thought we should proceed. I remember very clearly taking a pause before announcing, "I think we have to go forward with the meeting."

The gathering in San Diego was emotional. As a CEO surrounded by my top 250 leaders, I felt all eyes on me. I wanted to be honest and transparent, but there was still so much uncertainty about the hurricane recovery and the sale process. Furthermore, if the deal did go through, I didn't know if I would remain the CEO. As I stood on the stage talking about the company, with all the chaos swirling around me, I remember thinking, "This might be my last time on stage in front of all these people." I felt like I was marooned in a

> Ultimately the meeting was a powerful reminder that even in the midst of external disruption, chaos can be managed in ways that unite a team.

boat during a storm with little control.

Ultimately the meeting was a powerful reminder that even in the midst of external disruption, chaos can be managed in ways that unite a team. My insistence on maintaining transparency with my group proved critical in upholding stability amid the turmoil. The meeting also enabled our leaders to support one another in the middle of this natural disaster—even though the Texas operators were not there, everyone had remained so connected, it almost felt like they were. Every morning I started the meeting with an update from Texas. Operators on the ground would send pictures of what they were doing and convey their thanks for all the support they were receiving. During meeting breaks, every conversation was about the resilience of our teams. It really brought the company together at a time when we needed it most.

Through the hurricane and recovery efforts, our teams maintained extraordinary performance. Thousands of employees from the northern part of the state volunteered to travel down to ravaged areas and help their fellow teammates. Patients, employees, and family members slept and lived in the hospitals for weeks until power was finally restored. Operations were hurt, but the full effect of the massive storm on Kindred was contained. In the midst of uncertainty—with the hurricane's destruction, the company's ongoing skilled nursing center division sales process, and our key leadership not knowing what this meant for their future—our team remained united.

The only thing certain about Mother Nature is her uncertainty. Only thirty days after Hurricane Harvey hit Texas, Hurricane Irma tore through the state of Florida. Once again our preparation and determined, gritty workforce kept the company on track.

In the end, these two historic natural disasters, which caused enormous disruptions for our company and the potential deal we were navigating, only served

The first wave of Kindred volunteers going from Dallas to Houston to support those affected by Hurricane Harvey

to strengthen our resolve to advance. The result could have been otherwise. In the end, the potential buyers recognized that our organization's diligence to detail and incredible preparation demonstrated our strength as a workforce and as a company. Our response to these disruptions proved to be powerful incentives to acquire the company.

In the business world, companies and leaders pride themselves on being aware of and prepared for natural disasters and other unforeseen disruptions. This can go a long way. As we saw with our own response to the hurricanes of 2017, being transparent, supportive, and united can be the greatest defense and, in many ways, make a company stronger than before. With hurricane season winding down and the deal seemingly on course, I thought nothing could be worse than the acts of God we had endured. As a native Floridian, I was accustomed to nature being the ultimate disrupter—that was before I faced the complexity of the federal government as a payor for healthcare services.

ACT OF GOVERNMENT

Every fall, healthcare provider companies across the country—along with their government relations and regulatory teams—await what is commonly known in the industry as "rulemaking season." The Centers for Medicare & Medicaid Services (CMS), the governing body with oversight of the Medicare system, proposes updates to the reimbursement structure for each line of business in the healthcare provider space. In any given year, depending on the normal budgetary food fights members of both parties in Congress are having with one another, risks to reimbursement can be varied.

In the rulemaking season of 2017, all eyes were on the home healthcare industry. Home health had become the fastest-growing part of post-acute care delivery over the last five years. Despite previous attempts at rate regulation, Medicare spending on home health approached approximately the $20 billion level, and there were rumblings the federal government wanted to put a collar around it.

Parallel to the 2017 rulemaking season, Kindred was in the final stages of completing its four-party negotiation to take the company private, in hopes of changing its trajectory forever. After surviving the natural disaster disruptions of the brutal summer hurricane season, concerns were growing as rumors spread that CMS might lean in with a heavy hand when they issued their rule.

In October, word of the proposed rule came quickly and centered around a strange new rate structure called the Home Health Grouper Model (HHGM). HHGM was essentially a redesign of the entire reimbursement model that had been in place for nearly a decade.

Our initial analysis was frightening. It looked as though, without any changes, this was going to be a significant financial challenge for the company and potentially for the industry at large. If the proposed rule was finalized, the industry would face more than a $1 billion financial hit. Kindred, as the largest home health provider in the space, would suffer the most. The company would face significant financial disruption if this proposal was finalized. This not only posed a potential existential threat to the company, but it also clearly put the entire transaction in doubt.

Upon release of the new rule, home health publicly traded company stocks dropped in unison and without discretion. Kindred's stock price went down more than 25 percent over the following few days. Market capitalizations were being crushed all across the industry, as sell-side Wall Street analysts inflamed the situation with negative sentiment. I watched in disbelief as Kindred's stock price fell nearly in half, to below six dollars per share. I knew that despite all the difficulties we had overcome—despite truly believing the massive disruption our company would face was behind us—this act of government could potentially prove worst of all.

The deal itself was now hanging by a thread if we couldn't mitigate this external disruption. More importantly, I was worried about our forty-five thousand home health caregivers and the patients they cared for. If this arcanely constructed proposal were to be finalized, I could not be certain of their fates, let alone the future of the deal. To make matters worse, a proposed rule of this nature had a short window in which companies could respond through both political and regulatory pressure. A ninety-day window was all that separated HHGM from becoming law of the land. With no consensus within the industry on how to fix this disruption, it felt like we were down one run in the ninth inning with two outs and two strikes against us.

The following ninety-day period of advocacy would be some of the most intense of my life. With the deal as background—and the sanctity of our business as foreground—I set out to intentionally disrupt the disruption. Having been disrupted many times in the past by changes proposed in the rulemaking season, Kindred had developed a sophisticated government affairs engagement strategy. Not only did we have smart teams on the ground in Washington, D.C., we were strong members and leaders of the associations in which we served. In addition, and perhaps most importantly, I had worked tirelessly at developing relationships at the highest levels of both state and federal governments. Even though we had only ninety days for this specific issue, we had been establishing relationships and credibility in Washington for many years prior. We spent years and massive resources on public policy advocacy, relationship building, policy-oriented research, and other activities to ensure we had a robust set of tools ready to deploy when the time came—and it had come.

For every minute I spent with policy makers, my team had spent hours with their staff preparing content-based, policy-based, highly credible facts. Instead of just complaining, I was able to offer data showing how arbitrary the rule was and provide solutions including detailed legislative language. Using all the political muscle we could garner—after years spent developing trust and friendships on Capitol Hill—I personally rallied the CMS and HHS leadership, Office of Management and Budget decision makers, Senate and House leaders on both sides of the aisle, and even key figures in the White House.

My message was clear and consistent: This was the wrong policy, for patients, for families, for providers, for Medicare as payor, and for the healthcare system. I had a good policy position, and yet, as happens in Washington, after I made my pitch, everyone went silent. In the final week, I had a phone conversation with a senior policy maker. I made a final impassioned plea for help, but I couldn't decipher what the impending policy decision would be. Finally, on the eighty-ninth day of the rulemaking comment period, word came down from Washington that the proposal would be pulled and Kindred would live to fight another day. We had drawn a walk, put a runner on base, and now had to bring that runner home to remain in the game. The deal was still alive.

* * *

Over the course of 2017, I was faced with many disruptions, some foreseen and some unforeseen. Amid the chaos, I tried to remain focused on three major objectives. First, I had to manage the external disruptions, like the fallout from the hurricanes. I couldn't risk the lives of our customers or our teams. Second, I had to keep the operational train on the tracks so that the deal would not come undone, making sure our patients continued to receive the quality of care they deserved. Third, I had to navigate the complex policy-making process by utilizing all the analytical, political, and persuasive tools I possessed. I had to manage these objectives simultaneously, and since they all involved elements of internal and external disruptions, they were never static. Failure to manage any one of these disruptions would have been fatal to the deal.

While many moments of 2017 blur together, the one that remains vivid was making the decision to proceed with the leadership meeting in San Diego. I was torn between advisors voting to hold the meeting, and others voting to cancel it. Before making the decision I returned to what lay at the core of our business. It would have been easier to cancel the meeting and avoid the discomfort of trying to manage hard questions about the hurricane damage and the rumors around a potential deal, but that would have been contrary to the core. If the business wasn't secure and the patients weren't taken care of, there wasn't going to be any deal. If there wasn't a deal, the company would have been at risk. If a company chases a deal that impairs its core values, the business itself is impaired.

There is a line from the movie *A League of Their Own*: "The hard…is what makes it great." Though they were speaking of baseball, the adage applies to business as well. I ultimately went forward with that meeting because I knew it would be hard and uncomfortable, both professionally and personally. When I recognized this, I knew what I was supposed to do.

Any time you enter a disruptive environment, whether it's of your own making or thrust upon you, you can be confident there will be chaos and uncertainty. There's an old saying: "Doing the right thing is never the wrong thing." In the face of adversity, this was my compass. When storms raged around me, I returned to center by asking myself, "What's in the best interest of shareholders? How will it impact our ability to do the right thing for patients, for the business, and for our people?" At the height of external chaos, always attend to the core. A leader sees the chaotic storm ahead and goes forth willingly to stay true to their own core values and that of their team.

LESSONS FOR KEEPING YOUR BUSINESS ON TRACK AMID DISRUPTION

- Maintain communication, connection, and transparency.

- In the midst of chaos, return to your core values.

- If it's hard, it's probably the right thing to do.

CHAPTER 7

DISRUPTING THE DISRUPTERS

As the tumultuous hurricane and government rulemaking season ended, I was thankful no employees, patients, or family members had been physically harmed and that the home health payment system remained stable. Our hospitals and community-based operations had certainly taken a beating, but our core operations had held together, and our business prospects for the remainder of the year stayed intact. The hurricanes, of course, were not the only storms I was dealing with. The deal was gaining speed and beginning to show its true ferocity. The coming months would test my leadership in ways I never imagined possible.

While Humana had shown deep interest in a strategic deal with Kindred, the structure and nature of the engagement changed significantly as negotiations wore on. No longer did they want to buy the entire enterprise outright; they now wanted to partner with one or two private equity firms to simultaneously take Kindred private and then split the assets of the company after the close. Pulling off a deal this complicated would not be easy. It was hard enough to engage in a two-party deal where one side is the buyer and one side is the seller. With this many parties involved, we would essentially be solving a strategic Rubik's Cube.

Over the next few months, I was tasked with fighting battles on multiple fronts. I worked to find a partner for Humana to join its deal strategy. This would come in the form of two large private equity firms, TPG and WCAS. Both companies had shown interest in developing what would soon be known inside our dealmaking team as the "consortium." The board and I also continued engaging with several other parties, strategic and financial, that had expressed interest.

Most of these meetings took place in New York City conference rooms of banks or law firms, behind closed blinds. The "road show" process is one of the most intense and consuming experiences for a CEO. In total, I met with or presented to more than thirteen different interested parties. Each one performed their own level of diligence on Kindred with its respective armies of lawyers, bankers, and financial analysts. Many long days were filled with endless meetings and difficult conversations in darkened rooms.

On October 3, 2017, the new "consortium"—having watched Kindred's stock price fall precipitously on news of the previously discussed home health reimbursement rule—submitted a revised bid of $8.00 per share for the company. This was dramatically reduced from earlier written bids. After pushing back on this revised offer, the consortium responded with a new, albeit modest, proposal increase to acquire Kindred for $8.25 per share. I was displeased that after all the work we had done surviving the disruptions of the summer, I had begun to feel like the buyers were not appropriately valuing the company. I was prepared to recommend to my board that we call off the deal.

As news of the revised offer arrived, my lead financial advisor was on the other side of the world in Croatia. Despite it being three o'clock in the morning there, I explained that the revised offer was not going to work. After talking to the chair of Kindred's board, I instructed him to tell the other side that we were putting our pencils down once and for all. After nearly eighteen months of deal work—strategically repositioning the company against long odds and surviving a series of natural disasters—the deal, which had been on life support so many times over the previous months, was now dead.

After our phone call, I sat in my hotel room and considered all the disruptions we'd survived as a company and the personal toll it had taken on me. For several hours, I sat in that dark and quiet room feeling despair. I will never forget that night of introspection, reflection, and personal pain.

Early the next morning, on October 11, 2017, I was contacted by the CEO of Humana asking me if we could get together. I agreed, and twenty-four hours later we met in Louisville, Kentucky, where both companies were coincidentally headquartered. At this point, the thirteen other parties we had been engaged with had all dropped out of the race. The consortium, as flimsy as it was holding together, was all we had left. It was this deal or no deal—and no deal would be a tough reality for our equity and debt holders to accept.

As I walked down Fourth Street in downtown Louisville headed to our meeting at a local coffee shop, I considered the gravity of this CEO-to-CEO meeting. Not only was I in desperate need of resuscitating the deal for the sake of our shareholders; I was also going into the discussion with what felt like the weaker hand. On my walk, I reflected on all the events that had led me to this meeting. The disruptions had been ongoing, and the deal was now hanging by a thread. I decided it was critically important for our company that whatever message I delivered, and whatever outcome I derived, I needed to be crystal clear in my assessment of the situation and unequivocal about the value and position of the company. With this thought, I walked into the coffee shop ready to walk away from the deal.

I joined Humana's CEO at the countertop. After exchanging the usual pleasantries, I expressed my disappointment with the revised proposal the consortium sent several days before. I was frustrated by the length of time the diligence was taking. I expressed my concern about what felt like a weakened commitment on behalf of the buyers to push through and get to a mutually agreeable deal. I was clear and blunt: "Kindred is ready to move on."

For all CEOs, there comes a point when all the angles have been played and all the options have been run through. In this difficult position, there comes a point of clarity: the nuances fade away; the gray turns to black and white. There are no more options. This is it. When this happens, and your back is truly against the wall, you either give up or you punch your way out.

As I was facing this all-too-familiar position, Humana's CEO gave me a new set of terms to think about. He told me the consortium could raise their bid one more time, to $9.00 per share for the company. This represented a nearly 46 percent premium to the closing price of Kindred shares that day. He declared, "Ben, we can get to $9.00 a share, but we can't and won't go any higher than that. It won't be $9.01."

With the revised offer in hand, I had enough to go back to my board. The premium was significant, the buyers' desire seemed to be refreshed, and I knew what our board likely knew—this was our last and best remaining option to get the best deal for our shareholders. With this new offer, we weren't out of the dark corner yet, but it appeared we had made one important step away from it. Only time would tell if we would eventually be forced to surrender to a failed deal or succeed by punching our way out to a consummated transaction.

THE VOTE

As discussed in an earlier chapter, after the announcement of the HHGM proposal, Kindred's stock price fell to below six dollars a share. The resulting consequence was that the consortium of buyers had now lowered their bid for the company. After all had seemed lost, that fateful morning meeting weeks earlier with the CEO of Humana had pushed the deal back on track. Now, we needed approvals from multiple parties to get the final agreements complete.

Despite convincing the federal government to delay this painful reimbursement proposal, I did not feel much relief. In order to get the deal over the finish line and save the company from its massive debt load, there were still gigantic hurdles ahead. To sign a deal, we needed the board to vote. Once the board had approved the deal, we then needed to close the deal. The only way to accomplish that was with the approval of our shareholders through a shareholder vote.

The evening of December 18 would prove to be one of the most fateful days in the nearly twenty-year history of Kindred Healthcare. An 8:30-at-night board of directors meeting was called to take the final vote on whether to approve the proposed go-private transaction we had been working on for nearly a year and a half.

The room was emotional and reflective as judgments were rendered. Between December 2016 and this meeting in December 2017, the board members and the transaction subcommittee designated to work on the deal had met more than twenty times to review strategic options, dive into mind-numbing details, and consider multiple alternatives for keeping Kindred financially sound.

> Through all of the challenges and disruptions Kindred had survived, I knew we were one board vote away from making history and providing substantial value to our stakeholders.

The Kindred board had specifically focused on trying to create as much value for our shareholders as possible. In addition to the go-private deal on the table, the board had been evaluating for several months other options, including more divestitures, spinoffs, acquisitions, capital raises, and even new debt. No rock was left unturned in seeking the best available option.

Through all of the challenges and disruptions Kindred had survived, I knew we were one board vote away from making history and providing substantial value to our stakeholders. Each board member was asked to share their opinion on the final terms of the deal. As the long evening wore on, I was the final member asked to speak. I began by thanking each member of the board for their grit and determination in maintaining such rigid support for the company they had grown to love. For each of them, an affirmative vote to sell the company meant their affiliation with Kindred would also come to an end. Calling this meeting bittersweet would be an understatement.

I reminded the board of the obstacles we had overcome over the last four years. Amid all the challenges, our team of frontline caregivers and support staff stayed strong and dedicated. Because we sometimes lacked available capital and needed to conserve our resources over the last decade, many members of our team had gone without meaningful raises, and some had even endured benefit reductions and 401(k) match prohibitions. I got emotional as I considered all we had saddled our teammates with. We had cut hundreds of millions of dollars of overhead out of the company. We had reinvented the way that we were providing care. All the while, we kept telling our team that they could not let quality drop—they had to continue to care for our elderly sick patients and remain committed to Kindred's mission. My team never let me down.

Our chairwoman reminded all board members that their primary fiduciary duty was to protect the interest of our shareholders. I reminded the board that refinancing our balance sheet through this go-private transaction would lead to brighter days ahead for the company and our teammates. For most of our members, serving on our public board had become a vital part of their identity. It was something they loved doing because we were on the front lines changing policy and thereby changing the way seniors in America were cared for. The vote was tough because they had to essentially vote themselves off the metaphorical island. Each member had to vote with their values in order to make such a complicated decision. They had to do what was right for Kindred shareholders. "This is also a vote for our people," I told them. This vote would allow our teammates, and the patients and families they supported, to finally find the financial stability they so desperately deserved. The time for the vote had come; there were some heavy pauses and cleared throats. As morning dawned outside, Kindred Healthcare's board of directors unanimously approved the transaction.

On December 19, 2017, the headline of *The Wall Street Journal* read, "Kindred to Be Acquired by TPG Capital, Welsh, Carson, Anderson & Stowe, and Humana for $4.1 Billion." I finally felt the euphoria that I had desperately been seeking, but it was coupled with utter exhaustion. I hadn't slept well in months with all the challenges of the deal, the hurricanes, and the regulatory fights we had faced. With the announcement of the deal, and the Christmas holiday only days away, I looked forward to a respite with my family and loved ones in which I could reflect on the disruptive year we had experienced—and the disruption that I had intentionally engineered—and get some well-earned rest.

ACT OF GREED

One thing executives must recognize when they intentionally engineer disruption is that there will likely be a counterreaction to the intentionally disruptive act. Having survived an act of God and having managed an act of government, I now had to face an act of greed.

Two days after Christmas, and only eight days after announcing the deal with unanimous support of my board, a hedge fund and shareholder from New York called Brigade Capital Management came out publicly in the press to announce its opposition to the transaction Kindred's board had unanimously approved. Brigade declared it would exercise its right to vote against the deal when it came to the pending shareholder vote that would be necessary for the deal's final approval. The restful holiday I had hoped for was once again disrupted.

The last decade in the publicly traded equity stock market has seen a rise of "activist investors." Many hedge funds, individual investors, and analysts had grown impatient waiting out long-term strategic company improvements in favor of much shorter quarter-to-quarter earnings and stock price appreciation progress. The cultlike following of celebrity corporate raiders like Carl Icahn, Bill Ackman, and Nelson Peltz had made smaller "wannabe" corporate takeover specialists more aggressive in building their brands and shaking up the world of equity investing. The growing influence of proxy advisory firms, along with favorable Delaware court cases over the last decade, had made it easier for these small players to own only small percentages of a public company while giving them outsized ability to cause massive disruptions. Brigade was one of these new breed of hedge funds.

On March 19, 2018, Brigade issued a press release, with an embedded letter, calling on Kindred's board to reevaluate their membership and the members of Kindred's senior management team, including its CEO—me. "Rejecting the proposed transaction and taking a fresh look at Kindred leadership is the only step open to Kindred shareholders to ensure that their interests are protected," Brigade's CEO wrote in a letter addressed to me. I remember my dad called that morning and proclaimed, "I just saw a Google alert that a hedge fund is calling for you to be fired. That doesn't sound good." My response was, "No, Dad, that's *not* good!"

Brigade also filed a lawsuit in the Delaware Court of Chancery to prevent the shareholder vote, which had been scheduled for March 29. Needless to say, I was intensely frustrated with this latest disruption. It didn't seem fair, of course, to my team and our board that after such thorough examination of our options, years of intentionally disruptive offensive moves, and unanimous approval from the board, an investor who owned a small amount of the entire debt and equity in the company could so forcibly try to impede us. We had done everything in our power to create shareholder value, yet in this growing age of activism, for some, nothing ever seemed to be good enough. More specifically, our intentional disruption had now been disrupted. The lesson here? If you push all your chips in, you'd better be prepared for what happens next.

March 19, 2018: "Kindred Shareholder Opposed to Humana Deal Calls for Leadership Shakeup" (as appeared in *Louisville Business First*)

A major Kindred Healthcare Inc. shareholder opposed to the company's sale has called again for Kindred's board to reconsider the sale and also called for a shakeup of Kindred's leadership.

Funds affiliated with New York City–based hedge fund Brigade Capital Management—which controls 5.7 percent of Kindred's shares outstanding—said in a news release that Brigade continues to question the motivation of Kindred's board of directors and senior management as the company works out a deal to sell to Louisville-based Humana Inc. and two private-equity firms.

Kindred (NYSE:KND) announced in December that it had agreed to be acquired by Louisville-based insurer Humana (NYSE:HUM) and two private-equity firms—San Francisco-based TPG Capital and New York City-based Welsh, Carson, Anderson & Stowe—for $4.1 billion. The deal is set to close this summer and includes a $9 per share price as well as an assumption of Kindred's debt.

Brigade Capital CEO Donald Morgan III said in a letter addressed to Kindred CEO Benjamin Breier that the deal is "ill-timed" and "short-changes stockholders"; that Kindred conveniently revised projections for the company's performance more negatively just before the deal was announced; and calls on the board to re-evaluate its membership and the membership of Kindred's senior management if the deal fails to receive shareholder approval.

No other institutional investors have made public statements against the merger. So, it is unclear whether Brigade will be successful in its push to stop the merger.

"Rejecting the proposed transaction and taking a fresh look at Kindred leadership is the only step open to Kindred shareholders to ensure that their interests are protected," Morgan wrote.

Morgan also said in his letter that Brigade Capital is continuing a lawsuit in Delaware Court of Chancery that seeks to enjoin the shareholders' merger vote. But Kindred said in a proxy filing filed Friday with the U.S. Securities and Exchange Commission that the court has tossed out all but one of the claims in Brigade's case and has scheduled expedited discovery for the case on March 22, a week before the March 29 shareholders meeting.

Kindred declined to comment for this report. The general counsel for Brigade Capital Management has repeatedly told me the firm will not comment on its case.

In a comment for a previous article, Kindred's senior vice president of marketing and communications, Susan Moss, said the Brigade Capital case was without merit and expressed confidence that the merger will close this summer.

Kindred Healthcare noted that Rockville, Md.-based proxy advisory and corporate governance firm Institutional Shareholder Services Inc. recommends that Kindred shareholders vote for the merger.

When you choose a disruptive course—in this case, the proposed acquisition of Kindred done expressly for the survival of the company, employees, and patients—almost inevitably counterforces surface. Some disruptions, like hurricanes and policy changes, are totally external. Brigade, however, was the ultimate disrupter. They were taking action in direct response to my own intentionally disruptive plan. It's a high-stakes game, and if you're going to play, you had better have the stomach for it.

So what happens when a shareholder sues to prevent a deal? I was staring down a series of hurdles to gain a majority shareholder vote, win in Delaware court, and convince our largest equity holders to vote in favor of the deal. These had to happen in order for me to consummate what seemed like a lifetime of work. Proxy solicitation requires a vote, and I quickly became an expert in how many votes would be needed to secure the win. In a proxy fight of this nature, companies had to get 50.1 percent of the outstanding shares to vote for the transaction. That meant that a shareholder who simply didn't vote or forgot to turn in their ballot would count as though they had voted no on the deal. A massive effort had to be undertaken—the equivalent of what it must be like to run for elected public office.

Only a few companies offer proxy advisory services, the two biggest being Institutional Shareholder Services (ISS) and Glass Lewis. After meeting with management teams, boards, and dissenting share-holders, these advisors draft an independent third-party recommendation for whether or not a shareholder should vote for or against the deal. A lot of shareholders that own shares in publicly traded companies have particular guidelines that specify that they must vote the way the proxy advisory firm says they should vote. About 80 percent follow ISS, and about 20 percent follow Glass Lewis. We made a presentation to ISS to convince the proxy advisory firm to vote yes on the deal, which they ultimately did. Glass Lewis, the smaller of the two advisory firms, voted no. We were distributing public releases pointing to the ISS recommendation; Brigade was disseminating notices relaying Glass Lewis's recommendation. We went back and forth in the public marketplace. The campaign for votes was in full swing.

We could lobby each of our individual shareholders on our own as to why they should vote for the deal or not. In a collaborative effort with my board chair, we contacted our top twenty shareholders and gave them each a presentation showing how we got to this deal. We offered that same call to Brigade, but they declined. All the while, I felt like a politician running for election, trying to get people to vote in favor of the deal amid an increasingly chaotic environment. The energy in each conversation was palpable, and I had no clue if my efforts would disrupt the ultimate disrupters.

ARE WE THERE YET?

If this campaign had been the only thing happening in my life, it would have had my full focus; but as a husband and father of three, I had other responsibilities and concerns that needed my attention. For Kentucky families with school-age children, spring break is a celebratory affair. After a long winter, the annual break represents the arrival of warm weather, the thirty-day sprint to the Kentucky Derby, and for the Breier family, our annual ski trip. This year, of all places, we decided to ski in the farthest mountain from home in North America. It's one of the most beautiful places on earth, but it's about as far away from Louisville as you possibly can get. The flight from Louisville, Kentucky, to Vancouver, British Columbia, is more than seven hours long and covers nearly over two thousand air miles. The drive up the

Sea to Sky Highway to Whistler Blackcomb Mountain adds another two and a half hours. All told, it's a nearly ten-hour trip to get from the Bluegrass State to the Canadian Rockies.

Despite the lengthy journey, it was worth it to have some time with my family on the glistening slopes. Having grown up in the warm confines of Miami, Florida, snow skiing had not been a natural hobby of mine. Once I tried it for the first time in my early teens, however, I was hooked. When our children were born, my wife and I made a promise that we were going to teach our kids how to ski from the time they were little. Starting at about age four, each of our three daughters learned and developed their skills on the various mountain terrains across North America.

If you have children, you know that watching your kids overcome obstacles and achieve successes, particularly when they are hard-fought, is a powerful experience. Skiing a treacherous mountain without fear is one of the best examples of that emotional journey. Children have to learn to conquer extreme cold and sometimes difficult weather conditions. They have to learn the technicalities of making turns and staying in control. They have to persevere when they fall down, again and again. More than any other family activity, I looked forward to our annual ski trip the most.

As the shareholder vote approached on March 29, 2017, I was anxious to win the fight we had waged to take our company private. With our family's ski trip departure date of March 31, I hoped the vote would be closed in time to leave work behind for a few days and enjoy the much-needed respite with my family. The lawsuit filed by Brigade had wound its way through the Delaware Court of Chancery, and I was worried that it all might be in jeopardy—the deal, the vote, and the family trip. I hated the thought of missing this important time with my kids. The value I place on being "present" with my family supersedes almost all other external forces. As all parents understand, time with your young family is fleeting. I wanted to do everything in my power not to miss this important opportunity to be a dad.

After a contentious hearing on March 27, 2018, two days before the vote and four days before my family trip, the Delaware court formally denied Brigade's motion to enjoin the shareholder vote, ruling in favor of Kindred proceeding with its efforts. Out of "an abundance of caution," however, the judge determined that Kindred would have two options were it inclined to move forward with a shareholder vote. Option one was to delay the vote for a week, giving both sides more time to argue their cases in the court of public opinion; and option two was to open the vote on the previously scheduled time but hold the vote open for five additional business days. Option two meant the final vote tally would not be calculated until we closed the annual shareholder meeting on April 5.

Like most things over the previous eighteen months, nothing would follow a normal script, and nothing—not even travel with my family—would come easily. Disruption in business had turned into disruption of my family life, an all-too-frequent occurrence during my time as CEO. The rules governing an annual public company meeting are very specific. As the CEO, I knew I must be physically present at the annual meeting to officially close voting on whatever variety of motions have been made by the company that year. Most years at Kindred, the annual shareholder meeting was a quick and easy affair where the normal course of business was transacted, and the meetings lasted an average of about thirty minutes.

After conferring with our board of directors and our proxy advisors, we chose option two. That meant I would open the meeting on the previously scheduled date of March 29 but would need to be physically present on April 5 to close it. In the interim, I would be tasked with meeting telephonically with our largest shareholders to explain the rationale for the transaction and to secure the majority of votes needed to gain final approval to complete the deal.

The decision to hold the vote open for a week left me in a difficult personal position. I had spent the last eighteen months disrupting my family with my crazy travel schedule, unending late-night meetings, and rising stress levels around the house. I couldn't see how it made any sense to disrupt this sacred week with my kids, no matter what the physical costs might be. I made the decision to try to meet both sets of obligations.

On March 29, as scheduled, I opened the annual shareholder meeting at our corporate headquarters in Louisville, Kentucky. On March 31, my family and I flew to Vancouver, drove to Whistler, and settled in for the week. The next few days in western Canada were a whirlwind. In between trying to spend time with my family and portraying a sense of normalcy and calm, I was up early on the west coast making critically important calls to our largest shareholders. These calls required intense preparation and perfect performance. There was no room for error. I remember telling my wife what was at stake if I didn't get the votes: "I'll be looking for a new job. In this game, you don't lose and survive." She was eternally supportive, which helped, but it was a high-wire act. Both of us were all in. We had to be.

On April 4—not yet knowing if we had secured the necessary votes—I left my family at the ski resort, made the journey back to Vancouver, and flew to Louisville to close the shareholder meeting the next day. Ten hours and two thousand miles later, I was back in my office preparing for the final tally.

As the vote approached, we were making progress garnering the necessary votes needed for passage of our deal proposal. Each evening, our proxy advisory firm would tally the votes of the day and provide a running commentary of where we stood with the vote count. These counts changed numerous times each day, and I remember the analyst updating his computer what seemed like every sixty seconds. On one call, we were informed that our second-largest shareholder had originally voted yes but was now voting no. On the next call, after intensive lobbying efforts, it came in that that firm had flipped back to a yes vote. It was dramatic and constantly changing.

On the morning of the vote, I reopened the shareholder meeting under incredibly tense circumstances. Security at our headquarters was on high alert, as we didn't know whether anyone disruptive would show up trying to hinder our reading of the vote. At 10:15, the proxy solicitor announced the vote totals and declared we had achieved the necessary vote count to gain approval of the deal. On April 5, 2018, Kindred announced that its stockholders had approved the transaction by an overwhelming majority. I barely took a moment to celebrate before I mentally moved on to the next hurdle: closing the deal and splitting the assets of the company.

Thirty minutes after I banged the gavel, I was headed to the airport to make the colossal trek back to my family. I arrived in Canada late that evening, exhausted from the intensity of travel and the previous day's events. I tried my best to settle into our last twenty-four hours on the mountain before turning back around on April 7 to bring my family back home to Kentucky. In all, I took four trips from one side of the continent to the other. I traveled nearly ten thousand miles and spent more than forty hours in the air and in the car. I had accomplished both of my goals that week—I won the vote, and I gained my family's appreciation for keeping our sacred ski week intact. I faced massive disruption, and through sheer will, I had beaten it back.

On July 2, 2018, eighteen months after the initial meeting with Humana on that cold, rainy day in San Francisco, Kindred closed its deal to take the company private. Shareholders received cash at a substantial premium to our predisclosure stock price. The $3.2 billion of debt the company had accumulated was paid in full. In connection with the deal, the buyers elected to reduce the company's leverage. Our employees breathed a sigh of relief and could continue to focus on our patients without further distraction. The most disruptive and challenging two years of my life had finally come to a close. We survived Mother Nature, the government, and the disrupters to claim a new future, full of exciting possibilities. I had faced an act of God, an act of government, and an act of greed, and I had remained true to my core values and persevered through the disparate disruptions.

December 19, 2017: "Kindred Healthcare to Be Acquired by TPG Capital, Welsh, Carson, Anderson & Stowe and Humana Inc. for $9.00 Per Share in Cash"

LOUISVILLE, KY–December 19, 2017–Kindred Healthcare, Inc. ("Kindred" or "the Company") (NYSE:KND) today announced that its Board of Directors has approved a definitive agreement under which it will be acquired by a consortium of three companies: TPG Capital ("TPG"), Welsh, Carson, Anderson & Stowe ("WCAS") and Humana Inc. ("Humana") (NYSE:HUM) (together, the "consortium") for approximately $4.1 billion in cash including the assumption or repayment of net debt.

December 27, 2017: "Brigade Opposes Announced Acquisition of Kindred Healthcare by TPG Capital, Welsh, Carson, Anderson & Stowe and Humana"

NEW YORK (BUSINESS WIRE)–Brigade Capital Management, LP ("Brigade") today announced that it is opposed to the announced acquisition of Kindred Healthcare by affiliates of TPG Capital, Welsh, Carson, Anderson & Stowe and Humana, and will vote against a transaction under the current terms. Brigade believes that from the perspective of maximizing shareholder value, the proposed acquisition severely undervalues the company and ensures that the buyers–rather than existing shareholders–will reap the benefits of value enhancement the business is expected to generate from a number of initiatives and other factors. These include an improved regulatory environment, Kindred's divestiture of its low-multiple Skilled Nursing assets, the company's actions to strengthen its balance sheet since the third quarter of 2017, transitory disruptions to Kindred's business in 2017 as a result of natural disasters, projected improvement in the company's cash flow in 2018, the substantial completion of a repositioning of the portfolio and infrastructure in the company's Hospital Division, and the significant value of the company's net operating loss carry forward.

March 19, 2018: "Leading Proxy Advisory Firm ISS Recommends Kindred Stockholders Vote 'for' the Transaction with TPG Capital, Welsh, Carson, Anderson & Stowe and Humana Inc."

LOUISVILLE, KY–March 19, 2018–Kindred Healthcare, Inc. ("Kindred" or the "Company") (NYSE:KND) today announced that leading independent proxy advisory firm Institutional Shareholder Services Inc. ("ISS") recommends that Kindred stockholders vote "FOR" the transaction with affiliates of TPG Capital, Welsh, Carson, Anderson & Stowe and Humana Inc. (NYSE:HUM) (together, the "consortium").

March 19, 2018: "Brigade Continues to Oppose Proposed Acquisition of Kindred Healthcare by Humana, TPG Capital and Welsh, Carson, Anderson & Stowe"

NEW YORK (BUSINESS WIRE)–Brigade Capital Management, LP ("Brigade"), on behalf of funds managed by it, today released its letter to the CEO and Board of Directors (the "Board") of Kindred Healthcare, Inc. (NYSE:KND) ("Kindred" or the "Company") definitively stating its intention to vote "NO" to the proposed acquisition of the Company by a consortium of Humana, TPG Capital and Welsh, Carson, Anderson & Stowe.

March 21, 2018: "Two Leading Proxy Advisory Firms Recommend Kindred Stockholders Vote 'for' the Transaction with TPG Capital, Welsh, Carson, Anderson & Stowe and Humana Inc."

LOUISVILLE, KY–March 21, 2018–Kindred Healthcare, Inc. ("Kindred" or the "Company") (NYSE:KND) today announced that leading proxy advisory firm Egan-Jones Rating Company ("Egan-Jones") joined Institutional Shareholder Services ("ISS") in recommending that Kindred stockholders vote "FOR" the transaction with affiliates of TPG Capital, Welsh, Carson, Anderson & Stowe and Humana Inc. (NYSE:HUM) (together, the "consortium").

March 21, 2018: "Brigade Strongly Supports Glass Lewis Recommendation to Vote against Kindred Healthcare Merger"

NEW YORK (BUSINESS WIRE)–Brigade Capital Management, LP ("Brigade"), on behalf of funds managed by it, announced today that it strongly supports the recommendation by leading independent institutional investor advisor, Glass Lewis, to vote against the Kindred Healthcare's 2018 merger-related proxy proposals. In its report, Glass Lewis highlights its concerns regarding the questionable timing and unattractive financial terms of the transaction, as well as the excessive senior executive compensation that would become payable upon shareholder approval of the company's "Golden Parachute" proxy proposal.

March 27, 2018: "Delaware Court Denies Brigade Capital Motion to Enjoin Vote on Kindred Transaction with TPG Capital, Welsh, Carson, Anderson & Stowe and Humana Inc."

LOUISVILLE, KY (BUSINESS WIRE)–Kindred Healthcare, Inc. ("Kindred" or the "Company") (NYSE:KND) today announced that the Court of Chancery of the State of Delaware has ruled in favor of Kindred and its Board of Directors and denied the motion for preliminary injunction filed by Brigade Capital Management ("Brigade") regarding the pending acquisition of Kindred by affiliates of TPG Capital, Welsh, Carson, Anderson & Stowe and Humana Inc. (NYSE:HUM). With this ruling, the Court has denied all of the relief Brigade sought in connection with its motion for preliminary injunction.

March 28 Brigade release: "Brigade Corrects Inaccuracies in Kindred Healthcare's (KND) Press Release, Urges Shareholders to Take Advantage of Court-Ordered Extension to Voting Period and Vote 'no' to Proposed Acquisition"

NEW YORK (BUSINESS WIRE)–Brigade Capital Management, LP ("Brigade"), on behalf of funds managed by it, today responded to yesterday's press release by Kindred Healthcare, Inc. (NYSE:KND) ("Kindred" or the "Company") to correct what Brigade views as misleading statements by Kindred. Brigade believes Kindred's shareholders deserve better and should vote "NO" to the proposed acquisition of the Company by a consortium of Humana, TPG Capital and Welsh, Carson, Anderson & Stowe.

April 5, 2018: "Kindred Stockholders Approve Transaction with TPG Capital, Welsh, Carson, Anderson & Stowe and Humana Inc."

LOUISVILLE, KY (BUSINESS WIRE)–Kindred Healthcare, Inc. ("Kindred" or the "Company") (NYSE:KND) today announced that at its special meeting of stockholders, stockholders approved the transaction with affiliates of TPG Capital, Welsh, Carson, Anderson & Stowe and Humana Inc. (NYSE:HUM) (together, the "consortium"). The final vote results will be reported on a Form 8-K filed with the Securities and Exchange Commission.

July 2, 2018: "Humana, Together with TPG Capital and Welsh, Carson, Anderson & Stowe, Announce Completion of the Acquisition of Kindred Healthcare, Inc."

LOUISVILLE, KY, and SAN FRANCISCO and NEW YORK (BUSINESS WIRE)–Humana Inc. (NYSE:HUM), TPG Capital (TPG) and Welsh, Carson, Anderson & Stowe (WCAS) (collectively, the Consortium) today announced the completion of the previously announced acquisition of Kindred Healthcare, Inc. (Kindred).

* * *

Since the closing, I am certainly more relaxed about the company, about being in my own skin, about our future. For example, when the Texas Supreme Court recently declared that Obamacare was unconstitutional, the entire public company healthcare industry turned inside out. I got a note from a member of my leadership team that read, "Isn't it great not to be a publicly traded company today?" It was true—in these situations, it is assuring that the only people who need to know where we stand are my investors and my partners.

I often tell my friends and family that I'm working way harder than I thought I would be, and it's way more stressful than I want it to be. Many have responded that from the outside, it appears that I can create stress in anything I do in my life. Perhaps they are right. I'm not particularly good at watching the grass grow under my feet. I'm always thinking, "What's next?" The downside of being an intentional disrupter is that there is always another hurdle to clear.

The physics of disruptive leadership means that there are always counterforces at play. What disrupts will be disrupted back. The upside, however, is personal and professional resolve and tenacity. As an intentional disrupter, I will never be a Zen CEO. I will always be ready for the counterforces that seek to disrupt what I have spent my time and resources building. Intentional disruption is a strategy that carries risks. If you're going to be a disrupter, do so with eyes wide open because it isn't for the faint of heart.

LESSONS FOR DISRUPTING THE DISRUPTERS

- Be prepared for risks.

- Communicate about risks to key team and stakeholders.

- Compare risks of being disruptive with risks of being passive/nondisruptive.

- Be aware of counterforces that may disrupt you back, and be prepared to go all the way.

PART III

MANAGING THE EFFECTS OF INTENTIONAL DISRUPTION

CHAPTER 8

DISRUPTIVE LEADERSHIP IS A TEAM SPORT

IN 1982, THE *MIAMI NEWS* ran a sports article called "Baseball's Best Arms Die Young." The author, John Crittenden, was the sports editor of the paper and a longtime columnist. Though it never mentioned my name specifically, the article was written about me. In it, Crittenden lamented a ten-year-old boy, a star on his Little League team, who had broken his elbow because he had been asked to throw too many pitches at too young of an age.[12] The article gained national attention and began the growing debate about how much a young kid should pitch before he is fully developed.

---

12 John Crittenden, "Baseball's Best Arms Die Young," *Miami News*, May 11, 1982, 15.

John Crittenden
Sports Editor

Baseball's best arms die young

Charlie Greene, the baseball coach at Miami Dade Community College South, was at Sunland Park the other day to watch his son, also named Charlie, play in a Howard-Palmetto Khoury League game.

The opposing pitcher had to leave after three innings with a sore arm. The pitcher's arm was iced down to relieve the pain. "And they had the ice all ready," said Greene, "so they knew it was coming. It had happened before."

Greene thought that was terrible. "Sad," he said.

At age 11, young Charlie is an outstanding catcher, a unanimous selection to his league's all-star team. Since his arm is strong, there have been suggestions that Charlie should pitch. "Charlie says no," explained Greene, "and I say no and my wife says no. When he is 15 years old, that will be time enough for Charlie to pitch."

The Dade South coach is dead set against youngsters ruining their arms for baseball through early overwork or misuse.

"When they are between the ages of 8 and 14," said Greene, "we identify the best arms in the country ... and destroy them. Those who survive without being identified go to the major leagues."

The second-best pitchers of their generation are the ones who make it in baseball, Greene believes. That's strong talk. But Greene is certain that he is right.

"A healthy arm is more important than any amount of pitching experience a kid can get," said the Dade South coach. "And it's a lot more important to win at age 18 than at 14."

Coaches don't listen as carefully as they should when a player says his arm hurts, Greene contends. Pitchers themselves are reluctant to admit that they are in pain. "When a kid is tired, he goes to sleep," said Greene. "When he is hungry, he eats. But when his arm hurts, it's not manly to admit it."

Greene listens when his players complain. "The player tells me when he is hurt, I don't tell him. And I don't hesitate to take his word."

But somebody has to pitch in the kid leagues. "Let pitchers throw one inning a game, and no more," offered Greene. "That would hurt the quality of the play. But it would save a lot of arms."

The Dade South coach is not some loon with a grudge against kid-league baseball. He has been a coach for 25 years, his team won the national junior college championship a year ago and Greene is such a highly regarded student of pitching arm aches that he tours nationally to speak at clinics on the subject.

With trainer Terry Whieldon and Dr. Arthur Pearl, an orthopedic surgeon, Greene has written a book on the care and prevention of sore arms.

The book is dedicated to Gil Patterson, a former Dade South player who hooked up with the New York Yankees after college.

Patterson was regarded as the top prospect in all baseball in 1976, said Greene. "Rated higher than Ron Guidry," said the coach. Patterson hurt his arm pitching in the winter leagues that season. He is still trying, but hasn't gotten above Class A baseball since. At one point the man who had been able to throw 95 mph couldn't pitch a ball five yards.

"Had I known what I know now, I don't think his arm would have been hurt," said Greene. "Gil paid the price for my ignorance. I could have helped him if I had known a little more. I did my best, but now my best is better.

"It took me 20 years to learn the value of warming up."

But sore arms don't come about in a day, and Patterson's problems surely began long before he came to Dade South. Patterson never missed a turn pitching for Greene because of a sore arm. "I just wish we could have done more preventive things before he had to have surgery," said the coach.

The coach and his former student became very close as Greene worked with Patterson on his recuperation. "I'm close to Gil than any player I ever had because of the episode," said Greene.

"And Charlie [Greene's son] knows Gil Patterson like a brother. That's one reason he doesn't want to pitch at age 11." Patterson, a study of his history revealed, threw his first pitches in competitive baseball at age 8.

In contrast, Greene cites a pitcher who was on the Dade South team with Patterson in 1975, Jack Lazorko. "Jack didn't pitch until he got to junior college," said the Dade South coach, "and he has never had a minute's trouble with his arm. And he is in Triple-A, a hair away from the majors."

Greene was fascinated the other day when he read in The Sporting News that Smokey Joe Wood had been asked to throw out the first baseball at the Boston Red Sox opener and said that he did not know if he could do it because he still had occasional problems with a sore arm.

Wood is 92 years old. He hurt his arm in 1913, the year after he won three games in the World Series for Boston. And he said the arm had hurt on and off ever since.

"That's remarkable," said Greene. "But that backs up what I've been trying to say. Preventing arm injuries is the important thing. Once you hurt it, it never gets well."

Miami News, May 11, 1982

I wasn't worried about the national debate the article spurred; I was worried about whether or not I would ever play baseball again. After sitting out for nearly a year to rehabilitate my elbow, one of my coaches suggested that I alleviate my arm's strain by going behind the plate and become a catcher. At the time, it was a position not a lot of kids wanted to play. I remember putting on all the catcher's gear, sweating in the stifling Miami heat, and thinking this was a horrible decision.

Then something strange happened—despite the gear, the heat, and the squatting, I loved it. The position afforded me the prime vantage point: I could call all the plays and set all the defenses; I was the direct liaison between the manager and the rest of the team; and I was the one who could speak with the sometimes mercurial and temperamental umpires about various decisions and calls that were made. It is only in hindsight that I realize these were the same qualities required for disruptive leadership.

Through my teens and into my high school years, baseball—and being a catcher—provided me with a competitive outlet and helped to build my identity. One of the great things a team sport like baseball teaches you is how hard it is to find success without the help of others. This would of course prove increasingly true as I got into business, where—much like baseball—it is a team sport.

By the end of my junior year in high school, I had become an accomplished player who would likely have a number of options available to me after graduation. I was hoping to be good enough to be drafted and play baseball professionally or be good enough to earn a scholarship to a big baseball school like the University of Miami. I doggedly pursued both paths. Then, to my surprise, the head coach at Dartmouth College—the fine Ivy League school in New Hampshire—reached out to me to gauge my interest in attending school there. I had not given an Ivy League education much thought in high school. In fact, the idea of it had never occurred to me. I was a good student but not a great one; I was more interested in girls, boats, and baseball than I was in school.

As my senior year approached, the Dartmouth outreach turned into a waterfall of Ivy League interests. First Harvard, then Cornell, Princeton, and the University of Pennsylvania reached out with offers to attend their universities. It was pretty heady stuff for a kid from Miami who'd never even dreamed those kinds of schools were possible.

Despite being flattered by their attention, I didn't really want to go. I wanted to stay home and play for Miami. I wanted to be warm and live by the beach. My mother of course had different ideas. She knew the value of a good education and understood it set the foundation for a lifetime of successes. She wasn't taking no for an answer. "Pick whichever one you like the most," she told me, "but you are going to an Ivy League school, and we are not debating it."

After a difficult decision-making process, I chose to attend the University of Pennsylvania. I wish my choice was driven by scholarly goals, but in all honesty, their current starting catcher was a senior and was getting ready to graduate. I knew this would present an opportunity for me to start as a freshman. With a high number of returning players, I recognized they would have a strong team. Penn had been an Ivy League powerhouse for a number of years and had won consecutive championships. Like many decisions made in my youth, I ultimately chose Penn because of the baseball opportunities it afforded me.

Another prominent reason for choosing Penn was that the other schools scared me on a social level. Instead of fraternities, Princeton had eating clubs and Harvard had the Hasty Pudding Club. Frankly, I thought these were odd and too strange for a kid from the South. Penn, however, seemed "normal." It was in Philly, which was an enticing urban city. I thought I'd actually have an enjoyable time there, which was of utmost importance to me as a young adult.

Wednesday, May 17, 1989 — South Dade News Leader

Palmetto catcher Breier writes ticket with Penn

By RICH KATZ
Staff Writer

There was pressure for some of Dade County's graduating high school baseball players participating in the first Ball Buster All-Stars double-header Tuesday at Hialeah-Miami Lakes.

Some of the players — all of whom are seniors — were trying to impress the major league and college scouts in attendance one last time before the end of the school year. The teams were divided into the Red squad (the south) and the Blue (for the north).

The situation didn't bother Palmetto catcher Ben Breier. The whole experience was enjoyable.

"The pressure is in the district and the state champion-ship games," Breier said as he sat in the South's dugout during one of several rain delays which caused the first game to be postponed.

The second game was played and the North defeated the South, 7-2.

"The scouts have seen me," said Breier, who went 0-for-3 but threw out a runner trying to steal second. "I certainly would like to be drafted. But I enjoy being here with guys from different teams. It's a fun experience."

The pressure will come this fall, when he attends the University of Pennsylvania, an Ivy League school.

Breier, one of the best catchers in the county this season, and a key to Palmetto's success, opted to attend an Ivy League college and still play baseball.

Unlike most other colleges and universities, Ivy League schools do not offer athletic scholarships, Breier said. Student-athletes must work out individual financial arrangements with that school.

Breier did say he plans to take part in a work-study program, in which students work at jobs provided by the college or university to pay for some of their expenses. He said that would cover about half of the cost to attend the university or about $10,000 a year.

Tougher yet, he plans on enrolling in the prestigious Wharton Business School.

"It's not something I'm worried about but something I'm looking forward to," said Breier. "Balancing the academic, athletic and social life is a challenge."

Indeed, Breier is more concerned with preparing for a career but he still wants to play baseball.

"I had the opportunity to sign (a scholarship) with Indiana (University) or Georgia Tech," said Breier. "Since the ninth grade I have tried to get a balance between athletics and academics. When the opportunity presented itself to go to the University of Pennsylvania, I took it."

Actually, Penn was one of seven Ivy League schools Breier visited. Others included Harvard, Yale, Princeton, Dartmouth, Columbia, and Cornell.

And he visited them late in his junior year in an effort to gain early admission. As it turned out, the University of Pennsylvania stood out.

"It was the last school I visited," said Breier.

The visit took place last March where he met with University of Pennsylvania baseball coach Bob Seddon.

The school and Seddon liked what they saw in Breier academic credentials: Scholastic Aptitude Test Score (SAT) of 1,200 and a grade-point average of 3.70.

Seddon also liked Breier's baseball skills, based on what he saw in films of the player as both a catcher for Palmetto (.333 batting average, five home runs and 25 runs batted in) and

for the Cutler Ridge American Legion team — as well as recommendations by Seddon's scouts.

If Seddon liked Breier, the feeling was mutual. Breier was especially impressed with the campus, which is located in Philadelphia.

In September, Breier was notified he had been accepted at Penn.

"Fortunately, I picked the one I wanted," said Breier. "I feel comfortable. I really like the atmosphere. I love the location because it's between Washington and New York."

Breier is confident his choice was the right one.

"I wouldn't have undertaken it if I didn't think I could do it," said Breier. "I plan on enjoying all four years. If I can tackle these four years, I will be able to tackle challenges the rest of my life."

Breier added that the academic life and, yes, the quality of the baseball team were important criteria.

"This year, the Quakers won the Ivy League title and they're ranked 19th by ESPN," said Breier. "They got an automatic bid to the NCAA region tournament. Going to the Ivy League, you're not in the quagmire with other teams trying to get a bid to go to the regional tournaments."

Breier added that Seddon told him he would have an immediate opportunity to make the squad since Penn's starting catcher is graduating this spring.

"They're counting on me coming in," said Breier, who in 1989, batted .419 with two home runs and 29 RBI.

Breier is counting on the same toughness and discipline he has shown playing baseball to get through a freshman's fall semester, sometimes the most difficult time for an in-coming college student.

That's part of Breier's reason for choosing the University of Pennsylvania.

"It's worthwhile, "Just to have the opportunity to go to a school like this," said Breier. And, "Having a business background is good for whatever you want to do."

STAFF PHOTO BY AIXA MONTERO
Palmetto's Ben Breier turned his back on more glamorous baseball schools to play for the University of Pennsylvania.

South Dade News Leader, May 17, 1989

Once I made my college selection, I wanted to be accepted into the prestigious Wharton School of Business right out of high school. The baseball coach at Penn convinced me, however, that the easiest path was to begin a liberal arts curriculum and then transfer over. He made it sound simple and routine. Though that didn't turn out to be the case, in my naivete, I accepted his suggestion. I went to Penn thinking I would ultimately graduate with a Wharton degree.

Much like my decision to play in the Perrine Khoury League, my choice was not based on what would be the easiest path. In fact, one could argue that choosing an Ivy League school was by far the hardest option with the help of my "disruptive" mother. I was disrupting my idea of what I thought I wanted out of my college life to move to the cold Northeast and press my luck at a place I didn't know if I had the academic chops to survive.

COLLEGIATE LIFE

My first few years at Penn were filled with fantastic experiences. My freshman year I was the opening day starting catcher, and I continued to start every game that year. I was also named Freshman of the Year in the Ivy League and was a Freshman All-American. Our team went on to win the Ivy League championship, made it to the NCAA College World Series Western Regional, and I won an award called the Blair Bat, given to the individual with the highest batting average in the Ivy League that year. My sophomore year I was elected captain of the baseball team—an honor I would continue to garner each subsequent year. Even to this day, I remain one of the few players in Penn athletic history to be a three-year captain. A few years ago, I was elected into the Penn Baseball Hall of Fame, an incredible honor that reflects the time and success I enjoyed there.

In the early part of my Penn career, I was still thinking that I might have the opportunity to be a professional baseball player. There were a number of athletes who came out of the Ivy League and made it into the major leagues, including a few of them from Penn. For my first two years in college, I was focused on being the best baseball player I could be, which meant I excelled on the field but was average in the classroom.

After my first two years of college, I became more interested in what career path lay ahead of me. My mother and father had both been lawyers, but I knew I did not want to pursue law. Nor did I want to be a doctor. What was left? Business. I was aware early on that business seemed to be similar to sports because both allowed you to be a part of a team—something bigger than yourself. As captain of my high school baseball team, and later as a three-time captain of the Penn team, I understood that I had developed strong leadership skills. I also enjoyed public speaking opportunities at award banquets. My favorite aspects of sports, and the skills required for success, seemed similar to the traits of a successful business person.

As mentioned, I had been accepted into the liberal arts program at Penn out of high school, but with my growing interest in my future success, I wanted to matriculate over to the Wharton School of Business instead. The Wharton School of Business at Penn is one of the most sought-after degrees in the world. Despite what I had been told during the recruitment process, it's not easy to enroll out of high school, and it's even tougher to transfer over once at Penn. I had already researched the Wharton curriculum, and by the time I was a junior, I had taken most of the needed classes. I thought that if I took enough classes, they would *have* to let me in. How could they not? This was a precarious strategy because if I didn't get into Wharton, I ran the risk of not graduating because I had not taken the requirements necessary to get a liberal arts degree. I tried on multiple occasions to get in. Each time, however, I was rejected and told I shouldn't bother trying again.

For the first two summers of college, I was invited into what is probably the most prestigious summer league in the country—the Cape Cod Baseball League (CCBL). The league is made up of the top two hundred players in the country, who comprise ten teams. The

CCBL has been around for more than one hundred years, and most of the major league players today passed through its gates at some point in their careers. The structure today is the same it has always been. Players are invited to play, live, and work in the city of their team. Each player gets a host family and lives in that family's home while at the same time being given a job in the community. Players work in the morning, play in the evening, and "rest" at night, though there was rarely much resting in the CCBL.

My first year I had jobs mowing lawns as a golf course greens keeper, flipping burgers at Burger King, and pumping gas at a service station. My second year, I was the lead clerk at the local convenience store. The work was hard and the pay was lousy, but I learned an invaluable lesson those two summers on the Massachusetts coast: I learned about real work, about connecting to the people who ultimately make up the core of a company. The experience I had in the CCBL helped me learn to manage sideways in ways I never would have had without this amazing time.

> I realized that this transition wouldn't happen unless I intentionally disrupted the system, so I settled on a new strategy.

A player can only play in the league for two summers, so after my junior year, I didn't have a summer league to play in. Instead, I stayed at Penn to take additional classes I had missed due to the hectic nature of my baseball schedule. I knew this was the make-or-break window to either get into Wharton or fail trying. I realized that this transition wouldn't happen unless I intentionally disrupted the system, so I settled on a new strategy.

I decided I should go see the dean of admissions for Wharton to plead my case. As it turned out, the dean was a baseball fan, and

I often saw him in the stands at games. I was hoping this familiarity would benefit my chances of getting into Wharton. I went into his office and declared, "Sir, you have got to let me into Wharton. I've only taken Wharton classes. I'm not going to graduate unless you let me in." His response was terse: "That is your fault. You did that. I didn't tell you to do that. We have to see what your grades are like after the summer. Come back then." Instead of waiting until the end of the semester, I went back the next day. I said, "I think we should talk more about this." He reminded me that his answer was no. I kept going back every day. This went on for weeks. Each day I would pop in his office, "Hey, just stopping in again to see if you've changed your mind." His answer was usually an eye roll and an adamant head shake.

After about forty daily visits, the dean pleaded with me to stop coming to his office: "I will let you in. Just please stop showing up here!" I was elated and also had the sense—or was it the audacity?—to tell him I wanted to see it in writing. He pulled out my transfer form from the College of Arts and Sciences to the Wharton School that had previously been denied. With liquid paper, he whited out "rejected" and wrote "accepted." For the reason, he simply wrote "baseball." With that small stroke of a pen, my future was altered forever.

Acceptance form for the Wharton School of the University of Pennsylvania

To this day, that moment remains one of the proudest of my life. I hadn't just gotten accepted into Wharton—I had done it against long odds. I had persevered through a lot of adversity, and I hadn't been willing to take no for an answer. I had somehow figured out a way to disrupt the admissions process and force them to accept me. I had disrupted the status quo and gotten myself into the best business school in America. I understood that Wharton provided a great credential—I just had to figure out how best to use it.

During my sophomore year in the CCBL my baseball career was on fire, and I felt good about what the future held. The cape in the summer can be cold, and one fateful day I did not warm up well enough. I remember so vividly throwing a ball down to second base and feeling my rotator cuff pop as the ball left my hand.

I spent a lot of time rehabilitating my shoulder to get my arm back, but even to this day, it still hurts. My junior year, I tore ligaments in my ankle and broke my collarbone. After so many years playing baseball daily, I had broken and banged up almost every bone and ligament in my body. By the time I got to the end of my college career, I felt like I was a thirty-five-year-old man. My body was physically worn down, and I started to wonder how much more I could take. I realized that my dreams of playing professionally were dwindling, which meant I was going to have to make a living another way. That's how my baseball career ended—unceremoniously.

APRIL 22, 1993: "ARMED AND DANGEROUS: BREIER TURNS ADVERSITY INTO SUCCESS"

(by Steven Cook in *The Daily Pennsylvanian*)

When Penn senior catcher Ben Breier was three years old, his father, Bob, took him out to the backyard to play catch for the first time.

Not knowing how fragile his first son would be, Bob Breier picked up a baseball and gently tossed it to his son. When that didn't seem to bother Ben, he threw the next one a bit harder. Ben put out his hands to catch the ball—which proceeded to hit him squarely in the face.

"All of a sudden he realized it would be better to catch the ball than to let it hit him," recalls Breier, the elder.

A catcher was born.

The catcher's gear has often been referred to as the "tools of ignorance." From taking foul balls off the thumb or foot to absorbing home plate collisions with would-be run-scorers, catcher is the most brutal position on the field.

But if it's true what they say—if the mask and chest protector and shin guards really are the tools of ignorance, then for Ben Breier, ignorance is bliss.

"It's the only position on the field, besides the pitcher, where you're really in on every play," Breier says. "It really brings out some of the leadership abilities that I have. To be able to pick up the team when they need it and see everyone on the field. Nothing allows you to do that more than catching."

Leadership has never been a problem for Breier, even in his first year at Penn, recalls fellow co-captain Todd Wilson, Breier's freshman roommate. Back then the pitching staff was composed of four seniors who had been to the NCAA Regionals the year before and came within a game of the College World Series.

"From day one, Ben came in and basically dominated the pitching staff," says Wilson. "They were four seniors and he had them in the palm of his hand. He ran the show as a freshman."

Wilson remembers one particularly telling photograph that appeared in the DP that year. The picture showed Breier with his finger in the face of captain and All-American pitcher Craig Connolly, basically yelling at him to "get his act in gear."

"The strongest aspect is his leadership," Wilson says. "When [players] need to be yelled at he yells at them. When they need to be encouraged, he encourages them."

Much of Breier's ability to command such respect from his teammates so early in his career came from his outstanding credentials. Breier arrived at Penn from Coral Gables, Fla., as one of the top 10 catching prospects in the country. And he did not disappoint.

As a freshman, he won the EIBL batting title with a .500 average (.387 overall) in helping to lead the Quakers to a league title. One of Breier's most memorable moments as a Quaker came as a freshman when he hit a home run to beat 18th-ranked Cal-Santa Barbara in the NCAA regional at Arizona State.

"I can remember that entire week being one of the happiest weeks of my life, just being out at the regional," Breier says.

Hitting aside, defense is Breier's real forte. Earlier this year Penn coach Bob Seddon declared him "the best defensive catcher on the East Coast." As a junior last season Breier gunned down 27 of 38 would-be base stealers, a 71-percent clip.

"The biggest thing that we'll miss from him is his defense," Seddon said. "Maybe people don't realize it, but not many people try to run on us. That's a sign of respect. Against Cornell [last weekend], in four games I don't think they tried to run once."

During the summers of 1990 and 1991, Breier was invited to play in the Cape Cod League, perhaps the most prestigious summer league in the country. Sponsored by Major League Baseball, the 10-team league plays 50 games in about 53 days, basically teaching the participants how to be minor-league players. The experience gave Breier the opportunity to match his skills against those of the nation's elite.

"I certainly found out that I had the ability to play with the best in the country," Breier said. "It was a great honor."

Perhaps the biggest honor in Breier's career as a Quaker was being selected co-captain three consecutive years, a distinction he takes with pride and humility.

"It means that your teammates think you have something inside of you that when times are tough you can pick everyone up," he said.

"He's a game player," Seddon said. "He's very demanding on the field. He says the right things in terms of trying to remind everyone what the game means. And he's done an even better job this year because at times he's struggled. He was hurt and he wasn't hitting the ball a hell of a lot."

Injuries are nothing new to Breier. In fact it was injuries that caused him to become a catcher in the first place. Breier was a Little League pitcher like many of the good players at that age. But when he broke the same bone in his right arm twice from throwing so hard, he moved from the mound to behind the plate.

"The thing that shows me the most about Ben," his father says, "is that with all those injuries - broken collar bones, ligament damage, broken arms - he was always able to play."

Earlier this year, Breier might have suffered his most damaging injury to date. In a game against St. Leo's in Florida, he was involved in a collision at home plate in which he sustained torn ligaments in his right ankle. The ankle was examined by the Florida Marlins' team doctor at which point it was suggested that it be placed in a cast for 30 days to heal properly.

"My opinion of that was 'what's the next option?'" Breier said. "It didn't seem like a fair scenario. It was my last year that I was going to play here."

True to form, Breier instead decided to receive a shot of Novocain and play through the pain. Two days later, after missing only one game, Breier was back in the lineup.

"It was just a question of how much pain I could take," he says. "The ankle wasn't going to get worse. The team needed me and maybe more than that, I needed to play. I have a tough time sitting in the dugout."

The ankle severely hampered Breier at the Rawlings Tournament, at which several scouts were in attendance, likely dropping his draft stock. Although he has finally seemed to have shaken the effects of the injury, raising his batting average from a low of .180 to a respectable .261, this was clearly not the way Breier wanted his Penn career to end. The scouts, who were so interested early in the year, have all but gone away.

"He's in the right position," Seddon said. "He's a good receiver and there aren't many good receivers out there. But I think the injury did hurt him. His stats this year are not draftable stats. But as a defensive catcher and calling a game, yes, he has the ability."

"Anytime you put 17 years of your life and a lot of hard work and dedication into something, like I have, you don't want it to end," Breier said. "In high school my goal was to play at a Division I school. Now my goal is to just continue playing."

Somehow, you know he will.

FROM BASEBALL TO BUSINESS

By the time I graduated, my baseball career was over, though I did manage to graduate with dual degrees from the College of Arts and Sciences and the Wharton School. I did not have a job coming out of Penn. It was the early nineties, and the job market was tough. I had applied to virtually every company across the country looking for a way to start my career. Only one company was apparently looking for a broken-down catcher with average grades. I was offered a job as the assistant branch manager for a termite company office in a small town outside Philadelphia called Media, Pennsylvania. Needless to say, this did not thrill me. I wasn't sure what I was going to do, but I knew I wasn't moving to Media to be an assistant branch bug manager. I didn't have much of a plan other than wanting to return to warm weather. So I went home.

I spent the first month after college down in the Florida Keys with friends doing nothing. Then I went and lived with my parents. After only a few days, my mother approached me and said, "What's your plan?" This is a dreaded question for a fresh college graduate. I admitted that I didn't have one. She responded, "Well, you can't live here." I tried to argue with her; I mean, this was my home! She said, "It is not possible for somebody who has a degree from the Wharton School of Business to live at home with his mother. You have ten days." I asked, "Ten days to do what?" Her response was definitive: "To find someplace else to live." I argued that I didn't have any money. She counterargued that it seemed like getting a job would probably be a good place to start. "But I don't know what I want to do," I pleaded. Her rules were ironclad—I could visit, eat, and do laundry, but I couldn't live there.

After living on friends' couches for a while, I realized my mother was right: I needed money, which meant it was time to figure out what I wanted to do and find a job. Luckily a friend of a friend was the CEO of a hospital system, called South Miami Health System, that was looking for a financial analyst. I met with him, and he hired me. The hospital was in a big urban market, and he led a second hospital in a rural market in Homestead, Florida. After I worked for him for about a year, he asked me to transition down to their smaller hospital, Homestead Hospital, as it had recently been damaged by Hurricane Andrew. "It's really so messed up, I don't think you could make it any worse," he declared.

I was twenty-three years old, and he made me the assistant administrator and then the assistant vice president of Homestead Hospital. After two years there, I moved on to become the assistant vice president of Baptist Health Systems in South Florida. Two years later, I became the COO, then CEO, and eventually the director of premier practice management in Atlanta, Georgia. After four years, I transitioned to Concentra Health Services, where I served as vice president of operations for two years before advancing to senior vice president of operations. It was in 2005 that I was contacted by Paul Diaz, the CEO at Kindred. He wanted to recruit me as his potential successor, starting with the job of president of the Rehab Division, the smallest of the four businesses Kindred held at the time.

MANAGING RISK AS A DISRUPTIVE TEAM LEADER

Kindred Healthcare at its peak generated a little more than $7.5 billion in revenue. The company employed more than 110,000 people, did business in forty-eight states, and had more than 2,500 sites of service. As one of the largest companies in America, the size, scale, and complexity of running an organization this large cannot be overstated. To maintain any sense of execution readiness at a company of this scale, you need to build the right team.

It is difficult to separate my corporate leadership style and my baseball leadership style, because I have always found them to be so similar. Before I left for college, my father gave me a signed *Shoe* comic strip that made fun of the number of meetings catchers call in a baseball game. The interesting thing about the comic is that it applies as much to business as it does to baseball. Whether on the mound or in the conference room, there are a lot of meetings. The comic still hangs in my office today and serves as a reminder of the unlikely path that led me from managing a baseball team to leading a corporate team.

Shoe, by Jeff MacNelly, March 27, 1989

I remember seeing a catcher's "job description" in a 1989 issue of *Sports Illustrated*:

> *"Seasonal employment. Must crouch in the dirt, wearing heavy equipment for long periods of time. Must be able to catch hardballs thrown at 90 mph in unpredictable fashion. Must sometimes then throw a ball 127' 33/8" on a dime within two seconds. Must deal constantly with temperamental personalities. Must occasionally field a thrown ball at home plate, then stand in the way of a 200-pound runner who seeks to collide with the force of a runaway train." And you wonder why there's a shortage of catchers.* [13]

From my own experience on the mound, I would add the following to the job description:

> *Must take direction from manager, but be willing to make different real-time decisions on the field. Must position each team member in the right place on the field with sometimes limited information. Must lead by example, never show fear, and be prepared to defend teammates from angry batters charging at them.*

---

13 "Life at Home," *Sports Illustrated*, April 4, 1989, 18, https://www.si.com/vault/issue/702464/21.

As you can see, these descriptions are relevant on the mound and in the boardroom, and a similar skill set is needed to succeed in both roles. In addition to preparing me for the inordinate number of meetings, my baseball years taught me some critically important lessons about building and developing a great organization.

One of the foundational pieces to my leadership style is always to maintain what I call a "true north." An organization must be built on the bedrock foundation of its mission, culture, and values. In healthcare you often hear the phrase "Doing well by doing right." It is critically important, particularly during tough times, to know that the organization is built to accomplish the right objectives.

Jimmy Johnson, the great former coach of the Dallas Cowboys and Miami Hurricanes used to say, "I treat all my players differently." This was a bit of an anomaly to coaches who had always preached treating everyone on a team equally. What Johnson understood—and what applies to business as well—is that all of our teammates are motivated by different types of actions: some like to be pulled, some like to be pushed, and some like to just be left alone. My time playing baseball taught me how to motivate a pitcher, for example, who is struggling to get through the fourth inning. It was my job to know whether to pat him on the back and tell him it's going to be OK or start cursing and spitting in his face. The job of a good field leader, a catcher, or a CEO is to identify these individual traits and get the most out of the collective team.

As a team leader, you have to take a personalized approach when dealing both with your management team and your board. One of the things that I am proud of, particularly at Kindred, is the quality of the relationships I have built. These connections allow me to escape the CEO bubble and find out what's happening on the ground. With this vantage point, I am able to gain insight into a decision I might be pondering or the reactions to decisions I've made. These direct connections throughout the organization allow me to manage the team on various levels—by managing up, managing down, and managing sideways.

MANAGING UP

The board member's role is much like the team manager's. They ultimately make the decisions, but it's the catcher who is on the ground seeing things in real time and experiencing situations in ways the board cannot. For this reason, it is important to maintain active management through transparent communication and individual conversations with board members. These proactive measures ensure that when you need support or votes, the board knows and trusts you. Furthermore, a board is not a monolith. Its members, like members of a team, are a group of individuals and should be managed as such. A good CEO will develop personal relationships with board members to understand what really motivates them: some might be concerned with process; some concerned with price; some concerned with liability. Up and down the organization, it's these personal relationships that matter. As Jimmy Johnson understood, it's about knowing how to treat people individually and using the right motivators that impact them.

MANAGING DOWN

Managing down means making sure each team member knows their role and is positioned properly: a good shortstop should play shortstop; a good pitcher should pitch; a good center fielder should play center field. It means deploying each player in strategic ways that best suit the individual. This requires the leader to understand the strengths and the weaknesses of each player. For example, having made the intentionally disruptive decision to take the company private, I needed key members of my team to play specific and critical roles in the organization to ultimately get the deal across the finish line. I needed a CFO to brilliantly reimagine the capital structure and balance sheet of our company. I needed a general counsel to calmly and persistently manage the complexity of the transaction and litigation we faced. I needed operators who could execute their businesses without fail or flaw no matter how much noise was swirling around them. Literally everyone in the company had a role to play in the team's common goal. A leader must always lead but not always direct. Giving team members this freedom fosters independence and creativity, and it allows opportunities for other members to make key plays.

MANAGING SIDEWAYS

One of the best ways I've cultivated relationships with my team members is by not asking them to do things I myself wouldn't be willing to do. Never ask any member of the team to do something you haven't done yourself or wouldn't step in and do if needed. Getting your hands dirty and showing a willingness to be gritty are powerful motivating tools to push teams through difficult situations—a lesson I learned on many hot summer days working odd jobs in the Cape Cod League.

In the end, disruptive leadership, like baseball, is a team sport. Any leader who wants to manage risks in a disruptive environment has to have a solid and supportive team in order to survive. Much like a catcher on the baseball field, the CEO has to see where every team member fits best, direct the action, call the plays, and help manage a unique set of personalities around the mission of working together to achieve the ultimate goal of winning.

LESSONS FOR TEAM MANAGEMENT

- Maintain a "true north."

- Manage up—active management through transparent communication.

- Manage down—emphasize key members and clarify their role and position in the organization.

- Manage sideways—never ask any member of the team to do something you haven't done yourself or wouldn't step in and do if needed.

CHAPTER 9

DISRUPT YOUR FAMILY— IN A POSITIVE WAY

IT IS NOT SURPRISING that I possessed an innate drive to disrupt from an early age. I think many of the traits that have served me well in my life are a direct result of growing up in an environment that stressed drive and determination. In my family, you were expected to give the maximum effort in anything you sought to achieve, and failure to do so was not looked upon kindly. That didn't mean you had to win or be successful all the time; in fact, failure was a welcomed tool because it offered opportunities for growth. I remember my father telling me that a baseball player can make the Hall of Fame for hitting .300, which means that seven out of ten times, he failed to get a hit at the plate.

I grew up in a family environment where everyone followed their dreams with fierce tenacity. The Breiers were not a sedentary or complacent bunch. My father and mother came to Miami as newlyweds in the mid-sixties. My dad was an accountant by day and a law student at the University of Miami by night. He eventually joined a law firm for a few years before starting his own practice. Over the next two decades, he went on to build one of the most successful tax-focused practices in the state of Florida. Even though some of this happened before I was born, it was a part of the legacy my father impressed upon me—hard work is a discipline, and being out of your comfort zone can lead to enormous opportunities.

My mother was just as driven, as evidenced by her three graduate degrees. She was an ardent learner, reader, and teacher and took an avid interest in the betterment of others. When I was thirteen and my sister had just gone off to college, my mother announced that she had taken the LSATs, applied to the University of Miami, and would be attending law school. She worked for an appellate court judge of the State of Florida's Third District Court of Appeal, then became a full-time practicing attorney and ultimately a successful lawyer in her own right. Later she continued to push herself and invested in a restaurant business, which became wildly successful. She always challenged herself and never showed any fear about the unknown. She was the North Star of our family and had a profound effect on my work ethic and achievements. She demanded excellence but did so in an incredibly loving way.

My sister is also a force, and in many ways I've been following her trajectory all my life. She is three years older than I am but was four grades ahead of me because she skipped forward a year. Even though the space in our ages created little overlap in our social circles, she adhered to a daily sports-training schedule similar to my own. Whereas I trained in my batting cage each evening, she swam each morning. In fact, she woke at five o'clock to train year-round. She had clear ambitions from an early age and knew exactly what she wanted to do, which included moving to California and working in the entertainment industry. She moved to Los Angeles to attend UCLA and never returned. Her sophomore year she scored a summer internship with the Walt Disney Company. More than thirty years later, she's the Senior Vice President of Global Marketing Partnerships and Strategic Alliances, Promotions, Synergy and Special Events, making her one of the highest-ranked female executives at Disney.

The personal discipline of my family members and their attitudes toward work and excellence set the bar high for me—I'm a Fortune 500 CEO, and I'm the underachiever in the family! Luckily, I never questioned or rebelled against their high standards. In fact, I embraced them fully. It was just how things were done in our home. Creating a challenging atmosphere and maintaining excellence were the greatest foundations my family could have provided me. My family shaped me in my formative years and has continued to inform my personal and professional achievements. I take the standards that were inherent to my childhood home and make them an integral part of the home my wife and I have created for our daughters.

MAKING A HOME

At age thirty-four, I had been married for a few years, with a young daughter, Dylan—who was not yet two years old—and a second daughter, Cameron, on the way. I'd been living and working in Scottsdale, Arizona, for a little more than four years, but, as has been my pattern, I was growing increasingly restless in my professional position. I had been weighing a number of options when I received a call from an

> How could I disrupt my family but do it in a positive way? It was a question I would soon have to answer, and it's one I have wrestled with ever since.

executive recruiter about an interesting opportunity in Louisville, Kentucky.

For a guy who had grown up in Miami, Florida, with a wife who lived in Southern California and a current residence in Scottsdale, Arizona, Louisville was not exactly our view of paradise. It would be easy to disrupt my own life as a bachelor chasing down a living, but it was much more difficult now with a young family. How could I disrupt my family but do it in a positive way? It was a question I would soon have to answer, and it's one I have wrestled with ever since.

After the initial rounds of interviews for the job in Kentucky proved positive, I decided to broach the subject of a move with my wife. We were eating at the dinner table of our Scottsdale home when I sheepishly asked, "What do you think about Louisville, Kentucky?" Her answer surprised me: "What is Louisville, Kentucky?" She didn't ask *where* it was, because of course she knew the answer, but she couldn't understand *what* it was. More to the point, she couldn't fathom why anyone living in the paradise of Scottsdale would want to pick up their young family and move to Kentucky.

I tried my best to describe the opportunity I'd been presented with in Kentucky—the career progression, the professional development opportunities, the chance of real financial success. Her response was not surprising: "I know what's going to happen—you're going to get the job, move us to Kentucky, and we're all going to have to live in *that* place." Did I mention my wife was halfway through her PhD in counseling psychology at Arizona State University while all this was happening? Needless to say, the timing for my pregnant wife in the middle of finishing her PhD studies was less than ideal.

After two visits to Louisville, neither of which went particularly well, my wife acquiesced for the sake of my career and agreed to make the move. That meant we would move just in time for her to find a new obstetrician and deliver our second daughter—our first Kentucky bred.

As life would have it, fifteen years later, Louisville is still our home. Our third daughter, Hayden—also born in Kentucky—has joined our growing family and secured Kentucky as our happy place. We've learned that home is where home is. It's not the geography or the climate; it's not the ocean view or the farm view; it's being in a place where your family unit is the central part of your universe. Our family has thrived in this mid-major market in a way we may never have in Scottsdale or Miami or Los Angeles. We found our happiness because of a calculated risk we took to disrupt our lives and take a chance on a new and foreign environment in the Bluegrass State.

TAKING RISKS

The disruptive decisions my wife and I made have not come without costs. As I mentioned, from the moment I became a father, I struggled to find the balance between disrupting my career for professional gain and protecting my family from the disruptive counterforces that could damage their well-being.

Three times in my career, I have had to look my children in the eyes and explain why we needed security protection. This is an unimaginable position for a parent to be in. Knowing that you have put yourself at risk is one thing; knowing you are putting your children at risk is quite another. During the 2009 flag incident, I received death threats that required me to have police protection all day, every day. At the time, my oldest daughter was five. I remember her looking out the window and noticing the strange car parked outside: "Daddy, why is there a car there?" At her swim meet a few days later, she spotted the same man in the same car: "Why is he still with us, Daddy?" I had to explain to her that there were people out there who didn't think Daddy was doing a good job. This was a consequence and personal reality of my job.

On occasion I have held large political events at my house, and in the toxic political environment we are all living in, we needed to make sure we were protected. These are difficult concepts for my children to deal with. Explaining the realities of police escorts and secret service police on the roof and in the bushes of our house is complex and demands real honesty and transparency. Last year alone, during the early stages of the COVID-19 pandemic, I received countless threats from aggressive actors around our response as a company. The greatest crisis of our lives had only just begun, and instead of being able to focus on the enormous task at hand, I had to have bodyguards protecting my family.

Furthermore, because we reside in Louisville, where there aren't many public company CEOs, I'm in the press a lot. Multiple times a year, we are disrupted with a story about my compensation, job performance, or something personal and invasive like how much we paid for our house. Shelly and I work hard to gather our kids and prepare them in advance for whatever disruptive article might be forthcoming. We give them the facts, and we help them understand what they mean. We proactively prepare them to deal with any peers or teachers who might react to whatever is written about their father. We always maintain transparency with our kids about what they're going to see, what they're going to read, how people in their life might react, and how to handle it. We use this transparency as a protective strategy against disruptions.

I am an example of how the environment in which a child develops becomes an innate part of who they are and how they hold themselves accountable. For that reason, Shelly and I work hard to keep our children grounded. We discipline them and hold them to a high standard of public behavior. We encourage them to give back to the community through a series of service-related initiatives like feeding the homeless, helping foster families, and raising money for various charities. It's a broad and complex strategy that we feel our way through, but it always involves openness, communication, and holding our children to a standard.

These principles extend to the adults in the house as well. Not unlike most busy and successful CEOs, my calendar is one of the most complicated issues I deal with on a daily basis. The number of meetings, the nearly daily need to travel, and the amount of both personal and professional social engagements can be overwhelming at times. Add to that the frenzied schedules of three teenage daughters and their endless sporting events, recitals, and competitions, and you can imagine how complex the logistics can be. I try to balance it all— using part algorithm, part NASA space launch schedule, part luck, and mostly good, disciplined planning—but frankly, it's still chaos.

Time is important. Having a young family is incredibly challenging, but it's also the best time of life. I've made a conscious decision to disrupt my family and our already frenetic schedule by introducing a large amount of family travel time. It would make more sense to simplify our schedules and get into a routine, but I'm constantly challenging the status quo in our own household to get out, see more of the world, and develop unique family bonds that come from facing the challenges and adversity of travel. There's nothing more rewarding than banking the memory of an amazing trip abroad. Despite the disruptions, it's worth it to my wife and myself to experience history, see important sites and events, and operate together for days and weeks at a time.

Our family has made a conscious decision that disrupting our lives for positive team-building experiences is an incredibly meaningful part of our family plan. We come back tired, jet-lagged, and sometimes harried to make up for lost time, but we always have that warm feeling of accomplishment and togetherness. What I've come to realize is that I need it as much as they do, and it is as important to me as it is to them. In our disruptive world, the true source of my happiness comes from intentionally deciding to travel and make memories with my family, even when I feel like I don't have a spare minute. I want to memorialize experiences, and sometimes I must disrupt my family to do that. I think back on some of the things we've done together, and I wouldn't trade those experiences for anything. In the same way that my childhood environment imprinted on me, it is my hope that my daughters will grow up wanting to challenge themselves in new ways and cultivate a variety of experiences.

In addition to making time for travel, I try to keep my compass on "true north" when making my own schedule. I decided a long time ago that no matter how difficult my work schedule becomes, I was not going to be one of those parents who wake up ten years down the road full of regret for having missed their children's formative years. I work to manage my schedule so that I can get back home for most big events—games, recitals, father-daughter sweetheart dances. These are things I will purposely disrupt my work schedule for in order to attend. Oftentimes this means that I travel late at night or early in the morning. These sacrifices are worth it so I can consistently be present for my daughters as they grow up.

Of course my children aren't the only ones affected by the nature of my professional life—my wife is as well. Just as we hold our kids to certain standards, we hold ourselves accountable as well. Disrupting my family in a positive way doesn't always mean it's about me. Seven years after agreeing to move our family to Kentucky and leave her blossoming career behind, my wife was anxious to get back into the professional world herself. Based on a personal market view that our three young daughters didn't have nice places to buy girls' clothes in Louisville, my wife decided to start her own business.

I recognized this would be an enormous disruption in our family's routine. It's difficult to be the wife of a public company CEO, the mother of three busy kids, and active in the community on a number of different fronts. Adding entrepreneurship to that list was going to also add new disruptions to the family unit. Like most things in our family, however, we believe intentionally disrupting the status quo is the path to happiness and success. Because we set our standards for one another high, we all rallied around my wife's new idea and threw our support behind her new venture.

Armed with nothing more than a good idea, a business plan, and some capital, my wife opened FRESH Boutique 4 Girls in the fall of 2014. Nearly five years later, it became the go-to place for young girls to shop in Louisville. The store has been a tremendous success for my wife both professionally and personally. The experience has also helped shape our children's lives in ways I would have never even expected. Our girls get to watch their mother's success and determination with the same awe I felt when watching my own mother's. The girls also work the store almost every weekend, taking inventory, modeling clothes, and driving in new business. Perhaps most importantly, they see that hard work—combined with a good idea and a lot of creativity—can lead to successful outcomes. My children may not have gained those life lessons had they not witnessed my wife's intentionally disruptive act.

Disrupting your family in a positive way is not easy. It is a continual balancing act that requires openness, communication, and holding one another to high standards. Through it all, my wife and I have managed to juggle the schedule, the travel, the work, and the play to create a positive environment where disruption is welcomed and used for good.

When I think back to my own childhood home, I saw constant examples of maximum effort. It wasn't just a talk; it was a walk. I still think a lot about maximum effort and ways I can instill that in my own children. I cannot think of any better way than living the concept daily through the actions and disruptions my wife and I have made.

Each of my daughters has a quote in her room from *Star Wars* that references the seminal scene when Yoda encounters Luke Skywalker during his failure to lift his space ship out of the swamp. Luke tells Yoda, "I'll give it a try." Yoda responds, "Do, or do not—there is no try." This has been an overarching theme of my life, and I have this quote in my office and on my keychain. I lived it daily in my childhood home, and it's a legacy I hope to imbue in my children's home. Life is not an easy string of successes. It's a disrupted and chaotic mixture of successes and failures. The one thing that cannot be disrupted is the innate courage to continue.

LESSONS FOR MANAGING DISRUPTIONS AT HOME

- Maintain transparency and open communication at all times.

- Force yourself out of your daily schedule and encourage new experiences and initiatives.

- Be open to new possibilities.

- Challenge the status quo.

- Hold yourself and others to high standards.

- Don't let fear of failure stop you from trying new things.

CHAPTER 10

DISRUPT YOUR LIFE, NOT YOUR HEALTH

I wake abruptly in the middle of the night. I'm drenched in sweat. My heart beats erratically. What is happening? Suddenly a pain, a tightness, spreads across my chest. I can't catch my breath. I can't move my body. This is it, I think. I'm twenty-eight years old, and this is how it ends.

IN THE EARLY STAGES of my career progression, I was willing to disrupt my own happiness for opportunities that would advance my professional career, and it became a pattern I would follow many times in my life. Not unlike my decision to join the Perrine Khoury Baseball League when I was ten years old, I often took the intentionally disruptive path less traveled. This is how, at the young age of twenty-five years old, I became the CEO of what I would soon find out was a completely broken business.

In 1996, I packed my belongings and left the warm and friendly confines of Miami, Florida, for a job running the Atlanta Medical Clinic (AMC). AMC was a multispecialty physician practice that at its peak employed more than one hundred physicians, ranging from family practice doctors in rural Georgia—who sometimes took care of animals alongside human patients—to specialized cardiologists capable of life-changing surgeries. The first day I arrived in Atlanta, I sat in my empty apartment in Buckhead staring out the window at one of the few snowy days Atlanta would have that year. That glum day—missing home, missing friends, and missing warm weather—foretold the challenges and disruptions that lay ahead of me.

The AMC opportunity was born out of work I had done in Miami. In the early nineties, hospital systems across America had engaged in a new healthcare delivery strategy called "vertical integration." Hospitals started acquiring local physician businesses, employing the doctors, and professionalizing the operations of the back office. The strategy was to create operational efficiencies, present a more unified approach to negotiating contracts with newly powerful managed-care organizations, and hopefully, engender new and binding loyalties from the employed physicians to drive the ever-important referral of patients into the hospitals that so desperately needed the utilization.

In the mid-nineties, two publicly traded companies, MedPartners and PhyCor, had begun to corner the market by gobbling up large physician groups, using vast sums of their publicly traded equity as currency, and blocking the same doctors from practicing medicine at the hospitals they had used for decades. For the not-for-profit health systems in America, this had become a catastrophic problem. I had been tasked with buying and running groups just like this in my previous job at Baptist Health Systems of South Florida when the Atlanta opportunity presented itself.

A new company, formed out of a larger entity at Premier Inc.—one of the nation's largest hospital group purchasing organizations—had been created specifically to help not-for-profit hospitals fight back against this growing for-profit threat. It was this situation that had taken me to Atlanta in the winter of 1997. The AMC had been acquired by a large hospital system in town known as Georgia Baptist. Through a couple of different maneuvers, AMC also owned a network of primary care physicians throughout a ninety-mile radius around Atlanta. There was, however, one major problem when I got there: AMC was bleeding money. Financial losses were mounting. The situation was much more dire than I had been led to believe.

Three main things were wrong with the business when I took on my new role as CEO. First, physicians whose practices had been acquired had signed employment agreements that guaranteed certain levels of compensation without requiring any levels of minimum productivity. Second, the back-office consolidation had not gone well, and things like accounts receivable and accounts payable were not being met. Last, managed-care contracts had not been negotiated in a way that advanced the financial needs of the business, and it appeared every patient seen was actually costing money instead of making money.

At twenty-five years old, I was young and naive enough to not fully comprehend how bad the situation was. I was the CEO tasked with fixing the problems, so I couldn't run from them; nor could I wait for someone or something else to fix them. I had to attack. I poured everything I had into fixing this broken organization. I worked nonstop and around the clock. I took risks to try to solve big problems. I used every ounce of resolve I could muster to get the company back on track. At one point, three years into the process, I was told by my parent company that no additional funding would be made to the AMC. We were on our own. We would either find a way to cash flow the business without help, or we would put this long-standing medical group out of business irrevocably.

On a good day, being the CEO of any business presents hourly challenges. Imagine, though, waking up every Monday knowing you have a payroll to meet at the end of the week and yet knowing there wasn't enough cash on hand to fund it. It's a nauseating feeling and can become intensely personal. Most days, I found myself worrying about whether or not I was doing everything I could to fix the situation. I agonized about our teammates. I fretted about my reputation as a leader. If I failed at this, would I be viewed as a leader who couldn't solve the hard problems? Would it curtail my professional career objectives? The emotional toll was enormous and felt insurmountable.

One day, I woke up to find a rash all over my body. I thought I was dying. After numerous diagnostic tests and doctor visits, I was diagnosed with acute stress disorder. I couldn't believe it. I remember thinking, "I'm young. I'm strong. How is it possible that I'm making myself sick over the stress of this job?" I wish I could say that I had an epiphany and immediately began a proactive self-care regime. The reality, however, is that I was skeptical of my diagnosis, so I continued on as CEO, fighting each day to keep AMC afloat.

A year later, I woke in the middle of night covered in sweat. My body was numb, and my chest was tight. Again, I thought I was dying. I drove myself to the emergency room and underwent another series of tests. Ultimately, I was again diagnosed with acute stress disorder. I was twenty-eight years old. I should have been in prime health, but because I didn't have tools to successfully navigate the stress of being the leader of an organization, I was living with chronic, compromised health.

Over the next decade, my inability to deal with my own high-strung nature would rear its ugly head repeatedly. With each new physical manifestation of my internal stress, I was risking my own personal health and well-being, the happiness of my family, and my future goals. I could not seem to find a happy balance between the mental and physical rigors of my job. According to Steve Tappin,

CEO coach and author of *The Secrets of CEOs* series, "Being a CEO should come with a strong health warning: It's a grueling job and most chief executives don't have much of a personal life."[14] He goes on to report that after he and a neuroscientist interviewed hundreds of global chief executives, they determined that at least 90 percent struggled with work-life balance. It takes an enormous amount of energy to be a CEO. You're not

> This is a stark and sobering reminder that no amount of sheer will, mental acumen, or physical force will outrun the disruptive health risks of being an executive leader.

working a forty-hour week or even an eighty-hour week; you're "on" all the time. In order to be a successful CEO, you have to have the energy and the physicality. You never think about a job in which you are often sedentary, sitting in meetings, writing memos, and giving orders as something that is physically taxing, but it is. Tufts University cardiologist James Rippe has researched the link between CEOs and diminishing health. In a study of two hundred patients—75 percent of whom were Fortune 500 executives—he found that 73 percent were living a sedentary lifestyle and a high number of participants had high cholesterol, high blood pressure, and large waist circumferences.[15] That's certainly not the glamorous side of being a CEO.

Furthermore, a study by Stanford University's Graduate School of Business noted that, on average, seven chief executives of publicly traded U.S. companies die each year. Nearly half of the deaths (81) that occurred over a twenty-two-year period (161) came without

---

14   Steve Tappin and Andrew Cave, *The New Secrets of CEOs: 200 Global Chief Executives on Leading* (Boston: Nicolas Brealey, 2010), 21.

15   Martin Barrow, "Chief Executives at Risk for Heart Attack," *Raconteur*, October 3, 2018, https://www.raconteur.net/healthcare/chief-executives-at-risk-of-heart-attack.

notice. Nearly half of those (39) were the result of heart attacks. This is a stark and sobering reminder that no amount of sheer will, mental acumen, or physical force will outrun the disruptive health risks of being an executive leader.

When I became CEO of Kindred, I realized that being in such a high-profile, high-pressure job meant my health—like those of the CEOs studied—could potentially be compromised. I certainly didn't want to be a statistic so I vowed it was time to take action. I undertook my personal well-being training in the same way I approached my former baseball training. I needed to be in my best shape physically, mentally, and emotionally so I would have the energy to win the game but also have the stamina for the long season. Having been an athlete, I understood that I needed a training regimen to prepare for what I *knew* was ahead and also for what I *didn't know* was ahead.

I began to take an analytical approach to recognizing the stressors that had been negatively affecting my well-being. Previously I had not paid much attention to diet, exercise, and sleep; but now, in my early forties—dealing with the stress of being the leader of an organization and a father to three children—I began to study and understand these patterns. Since then, I've developed a rigid regimen of personal fitness and healthy eating. I work out with a personal trainer when I am home and use fitness gyms when I travel. I don't drink alcohol during the week, even when it feels socially uncomfortable.

Getting healthy and maintaining good fitness levels is not revolutionary. Small choices help to develop big habits. For me, being disciplined about my fitness and nutrition routines is a critical strategy for my professional and personal successes. These changes have helped me become sharper and better prepared to meet the rigors of being a CEO. It sounds easy and obvious to do these things, but as the statistics around CEOs and physical health show, it isn't always easily applied.

After proactively maintaining my physical health, my focus over the last number of years has transferred to my mental health. Developing a strong foundation for emotional and mental health is more challenging and is something I spend a great deal of time on. Admittedly, I still have difficulties with emotional pattern recognition, limiting stress effects, and working through anxieties. I've had to work much harder at this than almost anything else I've done in my life, and I confess, I'm still a work in progress.

There are a number of tactics I've tried over the last few years to intentionally disrupt my own ability to handle stress and stay grounded. Individually, each tactic is just a piece of a complicated mental health strategy, but taken together and applied over the years, they have helped build a foundation that allows me to better handle the difficulties that can come from being a CEO and team leader. My strategy includes psychological profiling, personal coaching, and the Human Performance Institute (HPI).

To highlight the leadership benefits of mental and emotional health, I have undergone psychological profiling of my internal biases, and I have encouraged those around me to do the same. There are many available tools for this, but my favorite is called predictive indexing (PI). PI has been around for quite some time. It's a test you actually only need to take once in your life for it to remain statistically valid. My results were very clear: I am a guy who likes to influence through taking charge, communicating effectively, and using my energy to persuade people to follow me. I'm not exactly comfortable as an extrovert, but I utilize the tools an extrovert would use to be successful. Sometimes using those personality traits that don't come naturally to me, however, can exhaust me, wear me out, and make me tired emotionally. My PI also clearly shows my key weakness: I am impatient—really impatient. I have to deliberately focus on listening and truly hearing what people are saying before answering them. I also have to consciously remind myself often to slow down.

PI REPORT RESULTS

Benjamin will most strongly express the following behaviors:

- Connecting very quickly to others, strongly motivated to build and leverage relationships to get work done. Openly and easily shares information.
- Strikingly expressive, effusive, and verbal in communicating; talks a lot and very quickly. Enthusiastically persuades and motivates others by adjusting the message and delivery to the current recipient.
- Very collaborative; works almost exclusively with and through others. Strong intuitive understanding of team cohesion, dynamics, and interpersonal relations.
- Proactivity in driving to reach goals while moving at a faster-than-average pace. Inquisitive about the world.
- Relatively independent in taking action on their own ideas. Resourcefully works around most obstacles blocking completion of what they want to accomplish.
- Eager for results; drive is for swift implementation. Works best in fast-paced environments offering a variety of activities rather than routines.

Summary

- Benjamin is an engaging, stimulating communicator, poised and capable of projecting enthusiasm and warmth and of motivating other people.

- Has a strong sense of urgency, initiative, and competitive drive to get things done, with emphasis on working with and through people in the process. Understands people well and uses that understanding effectively in influencing and persuading others to act.

- Impatient for results and particularly impatient with details and routines, Benjamin is a confident and venturesome "doer" and decision maker who will delegate details and can also delegate responsibility and authority when necessary. Benjamin is a self-starter who can also be skillful at training and developing others. Applies pressure for results, but in doing so, their style is more "selling" than "telling."

- At ease and self-assured with groups or in making new contacts, Benjamin is gregarious and extroverted, has an invigorating impact on people, and is always "selling" in a general sense. Learns and reacts quickly and works at a faster-than-average pace. Able to adapt quickly to change and variety in the work; will become impatient and less effective if required to work primarily with repetitive routines and details.

- In general terms, Benjamin is an ambitious and driven person who is motivated by opportunity for advancement to levels of responsibility where they can use their skills as team builder, motivator, and mover.

Management Strategies

To maximize effectiveness, productivity, and job satisfaction, consider providing Benjamin with the following:

- Opportunities for involvement and interaction with people
- Some independence and flexibility in activities
- Freedom from repetitive routine and details in work, which provides variety and change of pace
- Opportunities to learn and advance at a fairly fast pace
- Recognition and reward for communications and leadership skills demonstrated
- Social and status recognition as rewards for achievement

Self-awareness is a necessary tool that I lacked in my early professional years. It was my burgeoning self-awareness that ultimately enabled me to identify the tools that I needed in order to manage my stress and be an effective leader. The PI assessment is a mechanism for self-awareness and is the reason I require my executive committee and board to take it. Being self-aware of what renews me and exhausts me leads to a more rational understanding of what is affecting me at work and at home. I'm better able to give myself more of what I need and less of what I don't when I better understand these unconscious personality elements. This self-knowledge has led to a greater understanding of my stressors and how to navigate them. The second tactic I've deployed over the last few years is to hire a personal coach. Many people might think that takes it too far. The myth is that a successful CEO shouldn't need anyone to tell them what to do. They are like robots who are impenetrable and go, go, go. The reality, however, is quite the opposite. Tappin's research I mentioned earlier found that 50 percent of the two hundred global leaders he consulted for his book found their leadership roles "intensely lonely," with no one to talk to.[16]

Everyone needs someone they can talk to. A CEO has to find an outlet to share their apprehensions, frustrations, and aspirations in a place that is free from judgment. That's what I have gotten out of my coach, Scott, for nearly a decade. I've come to realize that this type of outlet is critical for my mental and physical health, and even though it takes time I may not ultimately want to give, I have learned I must disrupt my own schedule and routine to focus on myself.

The third tactic I used was a yearlong journey with the HPI in Orlando, Florida. This experience will remain one of the most important things I'll ever do in my life. I was introduced to the legendary founder of HPI, Jim Loehr, a few years ago. Dr. Loehr is a world-renowned performance psychologist and the author of fifteen books. In his books and teachings, he draws on more than two decades of work with CEOs and world-class athletes. In my favorite of his books, *The Only Way to Win,* he succinctly asserts, "One thing that matters is being alive, healthy, and present."[17] I could not agree more, and this is why I feel incredibly lucky he was willing to take me on as one of his last clients before retirement.

Jim taught me many things in my year of intensive observation and study, but the most important thing I learned was that blind pursuit of external achievement can often result in emptiness. We had many conversations that followed the same pattern:

"So, Ben, I heard you got a new car, a real fancy car. How's that make you feel?"

"I don't know. It drives fast."

---

16   Steve Tappin and Andrew Cave, *The New Secrets of CEOs: 200 Global Chief Executives on Leading* (Boston: Nicolas Brealey, 2010), 12.

17   Jim Loehr, *The Only Way to Win: How Building Character Drives Higher Achievement and Greater Fulfillment in Business and Life* (New York: Hyperion, 2009), 18, 29.

"Ben, I heard you moved to a new house, a big, fancy house. How's that make you feel?"

"I don't know. It's a nice house."

"You got a big promotion, Ben. How is that?"

"Well, it's fine."

"Ben, when is it ever going to feel good?"

I had always wondered why I didn't feel better each time I was promoted. I never felt fully whole after closing a big deal, buying a new house, or earning more money. Jim helped me understand that it's not about achievement; rather, it's the struggle and the challenges that come with accomplishments that make life worth living. He believes, as I do, that success comes from integrity, compassion, gratefulness, and optimism. He doesn't believe it comes from achievement itself. He says, "If success at external things doesn't really matter (to a great extent), then failure at such things shouldn't matter, either. What matters is the person you are becoming as a consequence of the pursuit, and character must be at the heart of everything you do and are."

I remember calling him at the height of my anxiety in recent years—I was working twenty-hour days, managing the Kindred deal, fretting over the company's future, balancing the board, uniting my management team, maintaining patient care, and trying to be a good husband and father. I called Jim and rattled off my worries: "I'm dying here, Jim. I'm dying! Everything is going to fall apart. It just can't go any worse than it's going." Jim was quiet for a moment, and then he responded in his gravelly voice, "Ben, you're missing the point. *This* is what it's all about. You're living, man. You're living! This is what you're going to remember. You're going to remember this, not if you succeeded or if you failed, or the next deal. You're living. You're living."

I don't know how he did it, but I remember hanging up the phone feeling completely unburdened: "Yeah, I'm living, man. I'm living."

I doubt I will ever fully become the man Dr. Loehr believes me to be, though I do try every day to think about what he might say when I am in particularly sticky situations. What I do know, however, is that just being aware of the importance of emotional and mental health is a good start. I've tried to balance the physical with the emotional to help build a stronger foundation for my health. I believe it makes me a superior CEO, a stronger father, a better husband, and it certainly has helped calm me down (some) so that it's easier to live inside my own skin.

* * *

As I reflect on my years as a leader, I realize that being the decision maker all the time can take its toll on a person's overall health. Truthfully, I went through a long phase of my career not acknowledging that lack of stress management can have physical manifestations. With the benefit of hindsight, however, I can accept it now. The reason I found myself in physical distress in my early career was that I'm an intentionally disruptive person. I was consistently putting myself in positions of high stress, beyond my capabilities. If I had allowed my ego to get lost in the achievements, if I had kept pushing myself harder each day, I would have lost all that I sought to build—my career, my family, my future.

Leaders are human. We are not impenetrable. Even for intentionally disruptive people, like myself, there are certain things you can't counterdisrupt. There is no greater disrupter than a health crisis. Having strategies to combat health disruptions is critically important to my success. Equally, these tools allow me the strength and mental clarity I need to be an intentional disrupter. After all, if what matters is truly the journey, as Dr. Loehr claims, then having the mental alacrity to appreciate the challenges and the joys along the way is a leader's greatest strategy on the quest for optimal health.

LESSONS FOR PROTECTING YOUR PHYSICAL, MENTAL, AND EMOTIONAL HEALTH

- Make your health a priority and approach it like you would a training season.

- Find a balance between the mental and physical rigors of your job.

- No one is immune to health crises—the greatest disrupters of all.

- The best health strategy is a proactive one.

- Seek outside guidance from mentors, teachers, and coaches to help manage the stressors of your career.

- Self-awareness is the ultimate tool needed to manage stress and be an effective leader.

- It's not about the challenges; it's about the journey.

CHAPTER 11

NEVER DISRUPT YOUR CORE VALUES

"Everybody has a plan until they get punched in the mouth."
—MIKE TYSON

THE PHONE RANG on a fateful Saturday in October 2009. It was my mother and father asking to talk with my wife and me about something important. Their voices on the other end of the line were somber and cracking. "I've been diagnosed with stage four esophageal cancer," my mother stated matter-of-factly. "I'll be starting radiation and chemotherapy immediately to battle the disease. The prognosis and outlook is cloudy at best. We are in for a very difficult fight."

Only a short four months later, my mother, Eileen Breier, passed away at the age of sixty-four. To say it was devastating for our family would be an understatement. The profound effect her illness and ultimate untimely passing would have on me personally—and in my professional path forward—would only be understood fully many years later.

As I have described in previous chapters, disruption—intentional or otherwise—has always been a driving force in my life and my career. I knew about disruption: I had used disruption to my advantage numerous times and had grown comfortable living in a disruptive environment. Despite all these disturbances however—acts of God, government, and greed—I had no strategy for dealing with the reality that my mother's life was finite. I had dealt with difficult personal decisions myself, of course. I had made tough calls. I had driven myself out of my own comfort zone. This disruption was altogether different, however. This was life and death. This was darkness and light. This was my mother.

This disruption knocked the wind out of me. My relatively smooth path to success had been turned upside down in an instant. I couldn't breathe. I didn't know how to come to work the next day. I had a hard time staying focused on anything other than the worry a child feels when facing the brutal reality of losing his mother. I was in that heartbreaking "in between"—I was an inconsolable child grieving a lost parent and a parent consoling three young daughters.

Anyone who is going through the difficult ordeal of watching a loved one, particularly a parent, battle an illness knows that the only true path forward is one filled with disruption. For me, my mother's sudden illness meant not only confronting the personal side of the drama but also figuring out how to deal with it professionally as well. In a moment, I went from being a senior executive running a complicated healthcare business to a man dealing with a healthcare crisis that was deeply personal to me in a way my job never could be. I went from helping people I didn't know navigate the burdens of our healthcare system to helping my own family in a time of crisis and personal disruption. The experience led me to a greater understanding of my own values and truths.

As the Mike Tyson quote so clearly articulates, just when you think life has taken you on a fairly smooth path, personal healthcare disruptions can obliterate your sense of certainty. The realization of how much time, effort, and emotion a family spends dealing with a health crisis was profound to me. It changed me forever—for the better—by providing me a centering point when dealing with patients and families at Kindred Healthcare.

My mother's illness, and its ensuing disruption, taught me a valuable lesson about the importance of navigating care. I came to realize that when people have a healthcare crisis in their family, it is not just about the care they receive. It's about clarity and understanding of what there is to do and who there is to talk to. It's about giving people the confidence that the plan they are following is ultimately the best plan for their loved one's successful care outcome.

This personal disruption in my family served as a valuable lesson in leadership, particularly for someone like me, who by design leads in an intentionally disruptive way. This lesson, which I carry with me every day, is to remain centered on my values—my North Star—in the midst of whatever professional challenges or disruptions I may face, whether imposed externally or internally. No amount of business savvy, toughness, or perseverance will result in long-term business success without being anchored in one's own core values.

My mother's illness brought home to me the important mission that Kindred and others in our sector serve: to help our patients reach their highest potential for health and healing with intensive medical and rehabilitative care through a compassionate patient experience. It also cast a bright light on the failings of our current system, even at Kindred, and how challenging it is for patients and families to get the resources they need to make informed decisions and find the right care. My values drove me to figure out better solutions to this national challenge.

When people have healthcare crises in their family, it's not just about the healthcare. It's about the whole process and the fragmentation of our system. It's about the lack of answers and direction. When I felt this after my mother's diagnosis, I revisited my core values. I realized I was in the unique position to create programs that could further assist families. It's not just about providing superior healthcare. It's helping people in a time of crisis and disruption.

As a direct result of my mother's illness and my own personal epiphany about the difficulties most Americans have in navigating the post-hospital—or post-acute—healthcare system, we created a business we now call Lacuna Health. Lacuna, which is Latin for *gaps,* is a twenty-four-hours-a-day, seven-days-a-week, 365-days-a-year nurse-led call center that allows any consumer dealing with a healthcare crisis to call free of charge and talk to one of our nurses or care managers.

Our teammates at Lacuna help navigate these "gaps" in care that so many consumers are facing. We refer people to the right places for information, for care, and for a support system. In one year alone, Lacuna representatives spoke to more than five hundred thousand customers, and Lacuna directed care to more than one million patients. What started as a disruption caused by my mother's illness has now turned into a business helping millions of people in need at their most vulnerable time.

LACUNA HEALTH USER RESPONSES

- "Your nurse went above and beyond to give me advice concerning my ninety-two-year-old mother."

- "I appreciate you listening–you took some weight off my shoulders."

- "Thank you so much for these resources. I appreciate you more than you know."

- "I was thinking about reaching out somewhere, and I needed something that has already had success–that's why I called here."

- "You have been the nicest and most helpful person I have talked to all day."

- "It's so nice to get answers so quickly and informatively."

As a grieving child, I recognized how important it was to take care of children who had lost loved ones. For this reason, I'm very proud of Kindred at Home's youth bereavement program, called Camp I Believe. As an extension of our former hospice business, this program is for children ages seven to seventeen who experience the death of a loved one. These camps are held in fifteen locations all across the country for thousands of children who have lost parents, siblings, friends, teachers. Their mission is to create opportunities for grieving children to come together and commune with other kids who experienced loss. We wanted them to have a place to share their stories and learn ways to manage their feelings. Camp counselor Nathan Bradley said, "We talk about everything from the physical feelings you feel to the emotional feelings you feel…A lot of [children] feel like they're all alone in this process. This camp teaches them that they're not alone."

Camp I Believe allows Kindred to have a positive impact on children whose lives have been disrupted by death. Our goal is to offer them tools so that, even in dark times, they can seek out light and hope.

STORIES FROM CAMP I BELIEVE

- "I'm here because my mom passed away from breast cancer. Sometimes I miss her, and I just start crying. She was funny, and she was pretty, and she was a really nice mom."–Camper, ten years old

- "I'm here because of my grandma. Every day I had off from school, every holiday, I always spent with her. She was my best friend."–Camper, sixteen years old

- "I know everyone here is going through the same thing as me, and I want to help them to heal like I did."–Camper, twelve years old

- "When I came to Camp I Believe, I was angry, and I didn't know that was a normal emotion associated with grief. I thought I was grieving wrong. I left camp with tools to deal with that anger. And now as a young adult, I still carry those tools. I experience new grief, but I have those tools at my disposal for life."–Previous camper turned counselor, twenty years old

In addition to Lacuna Health and Camp I Believe, I sought to do more to ease this disruptive period in people's lives. Based on my own experience caring for an ill parent, and my new perspective of the particular challenges and stressors this adds to a family's life, Kindred embarked upon a company-wide effort to measure how we are serving our patients and their families—not just the care they received but their *experience*. We use this patient survey to improve the overall healthcare experience, and we now build it into employee evaluations, compensation, and strategic goals.

Furthermore, when I took over as CEO, I decided to honor my predecessor by establishing the Paul Diaz Caring Award. This is an award presented at the Caregiver Summit, an annual gathering of two hundred of our top frontline caregivers in the country. Each year we get hundreds of nominees about our frontline staff, people who go to extraordinarily lengths to care for sick patients and/or their families. The Paul Diaz Caring Award is presented annually to Kindred patient caregivers who demonstrate an extraordinary sense of compassion and empathy while caring for their patients and honoring the lives of those who place their trust in us. These individuals approach their jobs not just as a means to a paycheck or the completion of their routine duties but also as an opportunity to make an impact on the individuals and families with whom they interact every day. These are caregivers who bring smiles to patients' faces when they are feeling down; who encourage their coworkers when they've had a particularly hard day; and who walk the floors of our hospitals, greet patients and families at our rehab facilities, speak to them in the halls of our nursing centers, and drive the extra mile to visit our patients at home. For our company, it is the most important award you can win. Not only has this been a wonderful legacy to honor Paul, but it is also a way for Kindred to lead with its core values: be kinder than expected; do the right thing always; stay focused on the patient; respect individuality to create the team; give your best; create fun in what you do.

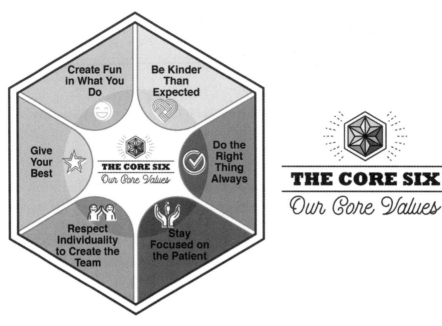

Kindred's core values: the Core Six

Our Kindred team members know that the only thing that matters at the end of the day is our values and how we treat people and patients. Our mission is a deeply felt need to deliver on the company's high-quality promise to promote healing, provide hope, preserve dignity, and produce value for each patient, resident, family member, customer, employee and shareholder we serve. When I am aligned with my own underlying values and the company's mission, I can remain centered and solid on my feet, despite the punches waiting around the corner.

> When I am aligned with my own underlying values and the company's mission, I can remain centered and solid on my feet, despite the punches waiting around the corner.

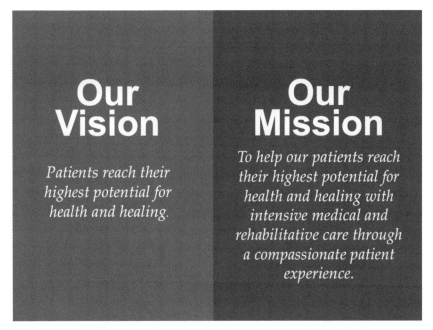

Our Vision

Patients reach their highest potential for health and healing.

Our Mission

To help our patients reach their highest potential for health and healing with intensive medical and rehabilitative care through a compassionate patient experience.

Kindred's vision and mission

UNCOVERING YOUR CORE VALUES

My mother's shocking illness and untimely passing taught me to honor my core values, both in my career and in my personal life. I am more aware than I ever was that life isn't a straight line in an upward trajectory. Disruptions happen, and when they do, they happen quickly. Becoming intentional about how to respond and rebuild was never more clear than in the wake of my mother's death.

It's not always easy to uncover and stay connected to your values, especially when disruptions, like health crises, can punch you in the face out of nowhere. This is why you must find ways to connect to your values *before* disruptions happen. There are two strategies I use to check myself against my core values: change my perspective and gain objectivity.

UNCOVERING YOUR CORE VALUES

1. **Change your perspective.** "The source of all truth and knowledge is in the building." This is a saying we often use around the Kindred offices, and it means that when you feel isolated, lost, or too focused on the wrong things, get out of your office and change your perspective. If I'm feeling too focused on business instead of patients, I'll get out of the corporate office and visit one of our hospitals. Inevitably, I walk out of those visits rekindled and reconnected to my core values and the vision of the company.

2. **Gain objectivity.** As we discussed last chapter, self-awareness is a precursor to success and a balanced life. It is also a powerful strategy for realignment with your core values. At Kindred, we foster this through the use of 360-degree reviews. These blind reviews allow team members to give and receive feedback from all sides, regardless of chains of command. We use this tool to connect ourselves and get objective feedback on how others perceive us—not just our personalities but what we seem focused on. If you get feedback that doesn't align with your core values, then you know you are off track and not living your values as well as you could. This level of transparency can sting sometimes, but objective feedback is one of the greatest strategies to track your core values.

* * *

My mother was a voracious reader and writer; in fact, I've never seen anyone read more than she did. When my first daughter was born, my mother wrote her a poem about her budding young life. Every month that followed, my mother would add another section, and at the end of the year, she presented her grandchild with a book of verses written to commemorate her first year. This turned into a tradition for each of my daughters. When my mother passed, my oldest daughter was one month shy of her sixth birthday. When my wife and I shared the news with her of her grandmother's passing, she looked at me with her little doll eyes and said, "Does that mean I'm not going to get my book on my sixth birthday?" Luckily my mother was also a planner and had completed the book before her death. This was a wonderful gift and allowed me to assuage my young daughter's grief. In that moment, standing in between my mother's death and my daughter's young life, I realized that some things are eternal. The books themselves might stop arriving, but the sentiments they held—and the foundation my mother built for me—was there for my daughter eternally.

For much of my life, I considered my mother my North Star. With her death, however, I realized that it wasn't her physical presence that guided me; it was the values and truths she instilled in me. These bedrock values guide me daily in my professional and personal life, and they are a direct result of my upbringing.

My innate disruptive nature comes from my family. Whether it was there all along or brought out by my parents, I'll never fully know. In my home, we were expected to shake things up. Whether that was by joining a new Little League forty miles from home or navigating New York on my own, my family always celebrated taking risks. Even going to a restaurant with my mother was an opportunity to disrupt. She never—and I mean *never*—accepted the first table offered. There was a joke in my family that "Breiers never accept the first offer or the first table." These subtle disruptions were built into my DNA, and I see them in my children when my nine-year-old politely asks waiters for a better table at restaurants.

Through her example of striving, risk-taking, and setting high standards, my mother dramatically impacted my life and continues to do so. In this way, her values live on in me and my children. When I lead with my core values, at the kitchen table and the boardroom table, I am continuing my mother's traditions. Disruption happens. We lose people we love, but core values stay as a testament to the legacy that will always remain.

Disruption without core values is a toxic mix. To be successful, you need to combine your core values with intentional disruptions. This is how you become an effective, value-centered leader. Anyone who is making a career choice, anyone who's faced with difficult choices, must make decisions that align with their values. Revisit your values often so that when you're challenged fundamentally, you can return to them as an anchor to deal with situations beyond your control. Intentional disruption as a strategy is not an end, and it will not work unless you're anchored in core values.

Oftentimes you don't even know when your core values are being established until much later. The same holds true in the foundations you are laying for others, like your children, your teammates, and your friends. When you lead with your core values and let them inform the quality of the work you do and the purpose of why you do it, then you are creating a legacy. This is why core values are so important and integral to every decision you make and action you take. If I can use my role as parent to raise children who lead with their values and use my role as CEO to build Kindred to lead with its core values, then I have honored my mother's legacy.

LESSONS FOR HONORING YOUR CORE VALUES WHILE EMBODYING THE SPIRIT OF INTENTIONAL DISRUPTION

- Painful experiences lead to a greater understanding of one's values and truths.

- Connect to your core values often and let them guide your decisions.

- Remain centered on your values in the midst of challenges or disruptions you may face.

- When you feel unmoored, check in with your core values by changing your perspective and gaining objectivity.

- Lead with your core values, professionally and personally, to create a lasting legacy.

CONCLUSION

WITH THE BENEFIT of hindsight, it's easy to look back over the last forty years and examine the pitches I called, the defenses I set, and the decisions I made. Retrospection provides a clarity that's nearly impossible when you are in the moment. As I reflect on the decisions and choices I've made in both my personal and professional lives, one thing remains clear: I have been making intentionally disruptive decisions since I was a child, and each one has brought me closer to my full potential. I may not always have realized the method behind my choices, but I've always clearly preferred the path less traveled. Once I recognized this innate pattern, I've purposefully used intentional disruption as a productive and winning tool to succeed in business and in life.

Using this strategy doesn't guarantee an easy path; in fact, it's quite the opposite. For every intentional action you take to counteract a disruption, counterforces will inevitably push back. From my own experience, I've realized that being intentionally disruptive for the sake of creating noise or chaos is not a winning strategy in the short or long term. Throughout this book I have answered a series of questions about what it takes to be an intentional disrupter:

- Are you an intentionally disruptive individual?

- How does an intentionally disruptive leader deal with the external disruptions that can upend an organization?

- When is taking aggressive, offensive action the clearest and most definitive path for an intentionally disruptive leader?

- How can an intentionally disruptive leader bring along others on their team to see the true value of changing the status quo?

- How important is it for intentionally disruptive leaders to maintain an organization's focus while pursuing transformative change?

- How can intentionally disruptive leaders manage their boards, shareholders, teammates, and other stakeholders throughout the different phases of intentionally disruptive organizational transformation?

- What strategies can intentionally disruptive leaders use to manage personal and family dislocations?

- What role do core values play in being an intentionally disruptive leader?

In the early stages of my life, I was faced with a number of intentionally disruptive decisions. Perhaps my earliest disruption was when I altered my trajectory by making the difficult choice to leave my comfort zone and join the Perrine Khoury Baseball League. I disrupted my life again by deciding to pursue an Ivy League education instead of the more comfortable confines of my hometown school, the University of Miami. In these early formative years, I was already answering the first of many questions: "Am I an intentionally disruptive individual?"

After considering my early disruptive actions, I offered guidance on how a leader deals with disruptive environments. Using real-life examples—like being pursued by the Department of Justice in a "bet the company" federal lawsuit and exploring a public relations crisis like the "flag incident"—we discussed strategies for *how an intentionally disruptive leader deals with external disruptions that can upend an organization.*

A skilled leader knows when to switch from playing defense and hunkering down in a bunker to playing offense and aggressively altering the circumstances and trajectory of a company. As I've learned, sometimes you need to intentionally walk the batter. The hostile public takeover of another healthcare services company is an example of taking the fight to the problem instead of letting the problem bring the fight. Leaders must constantly evaluate where their organization's footing is and ask the critical question, "When is taking aggressive, offensive action actually the clearest and most definitive path for an intentionally disruptive leader?"

Furthermore, we examined leadership skills and tools that CEOs must deploy during crises by asking another important question, "How can an intentionally disruptive leader bring along others on their team to see the true value of changing the status quo?" Imagine divesting billions of dollars of assets like Kindred did when we exited the skilled nursing business. Keeping our teammates focused on the task, focusing on the core business, and not getting distracted were all critically important determinants to the overall health of the organization.

Using an in-depth examination of one of the most complex merger and acquisition transactions in healthcare in the last two decades, we observed the challenging role held by an intentionally disruptive leader. The fight to take Kindred Healthcare private and the extraordinarily difficult leveraged buyout we pursued displayed *how important it is for intentionally disruptive leaders to maintain an organization's focus while pursuing transformative change.*

A seismic transaction like that of Kindred's full company sale demonstrates how complicated the dynamics become when multiple constituencies are involved. Focusing on the deal to take Kindred private, we examined *how intentionally disruptive leaders manage their boards, their shareholders, their teammates, and other stakeholders throughout the different phases of intentionally disruptive organizational transformation.*

Using my ongoing attempts to achieve balance as an example, we considered *what strategies intentionally disruptive leaders can use to manage personal and family dislocations.* We've examined different techniques—like transparent communication strategies, disciplined organization, a focus on being more present, and a willingness to focus on the journey, not just the destination—as keys to finding happiness both at home and at work.

Finally, and perhaps most importantly, we revealed that being intentionally disruptive just for the sake of change is not a winning strategy in and of itself. We must honor and revere *the integral role that core values play in being an intentionally disruptive leader.* Leaders can only be successful disrupters if they are focused on the change they desire aligning squarely with the core values of their lives and their organizations. In order to be effective, intentional disruption has to be driven by a strong set of core values. Only by leading with your core values will you find peace to live with your tough decisions and whatever results they may bring. You may win, you may lose, but as long as you are following your core values—your North Star—you will never be lost.

In my experience, if you're going to be an intentionally disruptive leader—one who uses a bold, purposeful business strategy to fuel opportunities and kindle successes while counteracting disruptions made by external forces—you had better have core values. Otherwise you are only creating chaos. You have to find your own way to connect with your core values, not just when major traumatic events happen in your life but in small ways each day, personally and professionally. I learned this from my family when I was a young player joining the Perrine Khoury Little League, and I relearned it over and over again throughout my role as CEO at Kindred Healthcare.

* * *

Whether you're the leader of a Fortune 500 company, a small business owner, a student, an athlete, or an aspiring entrepreneur, you are not immune to the disruptive world we live in. Everyone has experienced disruption, but not everyone has learned how to harness its power to fuel opportunity and kindle success. In the current business world, success isn't only about surviving a constant stream of disruption—it's about actively, thoughtfully, and intentionally disrupting the status quo using core values as your guide.

This high-wire act of intentional disruption is not for the faint of heart. It invariably comes with the reminder that leading with disruption results in inevitable counterdisruptions. The willingness to face these challenges anyway, even during incredible adversity, is the way to make intentionally disruptive decisions worthwhile.

Not everyone is an intentionally disruptive person, but all leaders at some point in time will benefit from this strategy. If you're not an innately disruptive leader—if you're not comfortable playing defense—rest assured, you can learn to. In the meantime, you may need to surround yourself with people who bring disruptive ideas to the table, because as we've seen in these pages, intentional disruption is a valuable business strategy.

Regardless of your current leadership style, sometimes you have to get out of your comfort zone and make difficult decisions and choices. During a class I took at Harvard Business School, professor Michael Porter said, "Not making a decision is in fact the same as consciously deciding to stick with the status quo."[18] Inaction in and of itself is a decision. You can't passively walk through life and hope that you're going to accomplish great things. I don't know anybody who has ever done it that way. In order to reach your full potential, you have to fight; you have to take risks; you have to choose challenges.

Sometimes you have to make your own luck. Sometimes you have to go on offense and be intentional about your trajectory. No one has a straight path to success. It's the trials of leadership and teamwork that create champions. When you win your championship, set a new record, or score the deal, you'll appreciate the challenges you overcame because those make the achievement worthwhile. It's not just winning for winning; it's the hard work and the intention to disrupt the status quo that makes it rewarding.

Some decisions are hard for a reason, and I promise that when you look back on your life, those are the moments that have the greatest potential to change your trajectory. The willingness to stand in and fight, to take on the emotional toll intentional disruption can

---

18   Michael Porter, "The New CEO Workshop" (lecture, Harvard Business School, Boston, MA, October 5–7, 2015).

bring to an organization and to a family, can only bring success if you are driven by your core values. This book shares the challenges, the mistakes, and the victories *this* intentional disrupter has lived over the course of nearly forty years. Success is not the endgame; nor is failure—neither condition is static. Instead, successes and failures are fluid reminders that real courage comes from perseverance and determination, and real rewards come from continuing the journey.

AFTERWORD

IF YOU HAVE completed this book, you now understand I don't like to sit still. I like to be on offense in all aspects of my life but most especially my professional career. It might come as a surprise that in the aftereffects of selling Kindred, I decided to stay on as CEO. Now, more than two years since we closed the go-private transaction, I decided not to further disrupt my family with another big move but instead to stay and help further transform all that I have built over the last decade and a half. As we learned throughout the book, disruption just for the sake of trying to appear disruptive is not a winning strategy. After the sale of Kindred, I chose to decline numerous professional opportunities so that I could see my family stable, happy, and where they want to be.

I can also now report, more than two years after the close of our go-private transaction, that we settled with the hedge fund that tried so desperately to hold up our transformational deal. For the first time since our board started talking about how to disentangle Kindred from its overloaded debt binder, the company is free and clear of hostile ownership elements. My decision to intentionally disrupt the Kindred enterprise through this complex initiative had finally drawn to a conclusion.

Not long after I finished writing this book, Kindred was settling in to 2020 with a renewed peace that all the foundational work we had done the past few years would lead us to a stable year of operational growth. Stable year? Not quite. In late February 2020, we heard of a novel virus spreading through China—COVID-19, a deadly disease that spread through the air. No one at that moment truly understood the global disruption that would befall us.

By early March, the entire world changed seemingly overnight. Like most Americans, I watched in disbelief as Tom Hanks, a global icon, announced he and his wife had contracted COVID-19. The gravity of the situation became clear when Rudy Gobert, a player for the NBA's Utah Jazz, tested positive and the league shut down virtually overnight. Closer to home, I saw the human catastrophe that occurred in a Seattle nursing home as the coronavirus ran through a skilled facility, killing elderly residents with brutal impunity.

Every one of you reading this book will have your own story to tell of how you navigated your family, your company, and your friends through this epic global catastrophe. Personally, I have wondered how an intentionally disruptive leader like myself can successfully manage through an unprecedented event like a global pandemic that has disrupted the economy, the healthcare system, social order, and almost every aspect of our daily lives. Throughout this book I have tried to transparently reflect on personal and professional examples of disruption and how being intentionally disruptive can counterbalance some of these forces. Even so, I was unprepared for how close to home this global disruption would hit.

In late March, just as travel across the country was beginning to shut down, my wife returned from a trip to Miami not feeling well. The pandemic was still so new to the national consciousness that we weren't overly worried. For the sake of certainty, she was tested, and several days later she learned she was positive for COVID-19. A mere inconvenience in our minds had now hit close to home with the reality that COVID-19 could get all the way to our own front door.

After she quarantined and recovered, I was thankful to have my family healthy and safe, but the experience in my own personal life created an even more urgent awareness of how this pandemic would affect my professional life. I knew this was going to be difficult, and I needed to be very intentional about the steps I was going to take to secure my business, my teammates, and my family.

I had three urgent initiatives I needed to make sure were met successfully upon the outbreak of COVID-19. First, I had to get my team to create a virtual corporate support center almost overnight. Second, I had to make sure our balance sheet was sound, with ample liquidity to make it through any secondary disruptions. Third, we had to shore up our supply chain, making sure we could protect our frontline teammates with ample amounts of personal protective equipment like gloves, masks, ventilators, and more.

We learned quickly that parts of the healthcare system were going to be irreparably hit. Some aspects might never be the same. As hospitals all across the country were mandated to discontinue taking any elective procedures, we watched in horror as they struggled to meet the massive care needs of the American public while hemorrhaging financially to the point of nearly going out of business.

As I shared in the book, I do my best to stay as calm and predictable as I can during times of great stress. The early stages of dealing with this terrible virus, however, tested me in dramatic ways. Using the decades of experience dealing with enormous headwinds and challenges, I've tried to attack this crisis in a similar fashion. At Kindred, we immediately assessed our situation to try to determine whether the humanitarian and financial repercussions of the crisis would affect us as badly as it did many in the healthcare ecosystem. We needed to pro-actively find ways to become a part of the solution to this pandemic, adding value wherever we could.

As it turns out, our specialty hospitals have become an invaluable partner and solution to caring for so many vulnerable Americans that have come in contact with this insidious disease. Almost immediately we set out to proactively manage the massive disruption in the flow of patients into our country's hospital systems, which looked at times like it would overflow the capacity of hospital beds available to care for those in need.

Kindred spent years developing protocols and skills necessary to take care of patients with illnesses similar to the coronavirus. We had the ability to treat people with multiple systems failures and infectious diseases and those requiring mechanical ventilation to breathe. We are an expert in dealing with patients suffering from strokes, neuro-rehab-related difficulties, and other conditions this terrible virus has inflicted on so many.

Our hospitals began serving as an outlet to free up the bottle-necks occurring in the emergency rooms and intensive care units across the country. We became an unprecedented partner to payors, providers, and families in need of care. We put ourselves in a position to be helpful in this time of national crisis because we had been very intentional to invest in areas where our partners needed us the most.

We relied heavily on team transparency, family, and our core values to push back on the disruption we have been dealing with. All the themes I have been describing in this book have been brought home to fight this virus.

None of us knows exactly how this will turn out. We don't know when our lives will return to normal. What I do know is that I will continue to play offense and intentionally disrupt to survive.

I will continue to work each day to preserve what this disease seeks to destroy. Will this finally have a happy ending? Stay tuned for my next book to see how it all plays out.

ACKNOWLEDGMENTS

THIS BOOK IS a leadership survival guide for everyone going through a stressful and undetermined outcome. Be it a management decision, an athletic event, a school challenge, or dealing with health, life, and death, I hope this book describes a path forward for everyone who reads it.

The idea of taking the narrative of my life, and coining the phrase "intentional disruption," emanated directly from a brainstorming session with my dear friend, advisor, partner, and collaborator William Altman. Without Bill's tireless efforts, vision, writing, and organizational skills, this book would never have been possible. To him, all credit is due.

Susan Moss is the finest marketing, communications, and public relations executive I have ever known. Her tireless efforts to see a finished product that we could all be happy with (and that passed her extraordinarily high levels of acceptance) made this book what it is visually today. Dawn Knight, Jason Laughlin, and the rest of the team at Kindred were incredibly helpful and creative throughout. I am indebted to their hard work.

Neeli Bendapudi, Jim Loehr, and my idol Johnny Bench all took time out of their busy lives to read the book, offer advice, and endorse its content willingly. I am so grateful to these three powerhouses for doing so.

Jeffrey Sonnenfeld and Jeff Cohn from Yale and Harvard respectively have always been such supportive mentors in this process. I learn more from Dr. Sonnenfeld's CEO summits than any other gathering I attend throughout the year. Jeff Cohn is an exceptional writer and a leadership icon when it comes to understanding CEO behavior and succession issues. His friendship and guidance on this project and many others cannot be overstated.

Paul Diaz, my predecessor and mentor, taught me how to become a public company CEO. He didn't have to do it. He didn't need to do it. He saw in me, I think, some of himself. That in turn made him want to guide my career progression. To him, and his wife, Viki, I am eternally grateful.

To my wife, Shelly, I simply acknowledge I am not me without you. Your guidance, love, and absolute steadfast tenacity in your care for me and our three children is the foundation of what makes everything in my life good. I love you.

Dylan, Cameron, and Hayden, my three daughters, you give me inspiration and motivation every day to do right, be responsible, help in our community, and try to make the world a little better place than we found it.

Lastly, to my father, Bob. RGB, you are the father that all fathers (myself the most) should emulate. You are loving but tough, you are generous and determined to do right for others. The unyielding love you showed my sister, Lylle, and me throughout our lives reminds us of what is truly important. Family always came first for you, no matter how busy you were. Watching you love my three children and their cousin, Jake, is all the lessons of leadership any of us need to see in setting ourselves on the right path.